# FOR THE LOVE OF
# SHAKESPEARE

FOR THE LOVE OF SHAKESPEARE

Summersdale Publishers Ltd
46 West Street
Chichester
West Sussex
PO19 1RP
UK

www.summersdale.com

Printed and bound in the Czech Republic

ISBN: 978-1-84953-925-8

Substantial discounts on bulk quantities of Summersdale books are available to corporations, professional associations and other organisations. For details contact Nicky Douglas by telephone: +44 (0) 1243 756902, fax: +44 (0) 1243 786300 or email: nicky@summersdale.com.

# FOR THE LOVE OF
# SHAKESPEARE

## A COMPANION

BETH MILLER

# CONTENTS

# FOREWORD

BY PROFESSOR MICHAEL DOBSON

DIRECTOR OF THE SHAKESPEARE
INSTITUTE, STRATFORD-UPON-AVON

The flourishing of Shakespeare's plays worldwide across the last four centuries – as they have gone on passing into new editions, into new languages, into new media, and into the lives and imaginations of successive new generations of readers and spectators – begins with something extraordinary done for the love of Shakespeare. In early 1616, Shakespeare made a draft of his will, and that March, probably knowing his death was near, he updated and signed it. Among its bequests, the will specifies that each of his closest theatrical colleagues – Richard Burbage, John Heminges and Henry Condell – is to receive twenty-six shillings and eightpence with which to buy a gold mourning ring. This seems to have been an established custom among members of Shakespeare's acting troupe, the King's Men: survivors would remember their companions by wearing rings in their memory for the rest of their lives.

For these particular three actors, though, remembering Shakespeare themselves wasn't enough: they wanted to make sure the world remembered him too. In 1616, another member of the company, Ben Jonson, was taking the unprecedented step of publishing not just his own poems but his plays in a big, expensive folio volume, giving his drama a literary status which no mere English playscripts had ever enjoyed before. Convinced that Shakespeare's plays deserved the same honour, Burbage, Heminges and Condell set about the huge administrative task of gathering together as many as they could of the plays which Shakespeare had written (some of them by now a quarter of a century old), of negotiating about copyright with the printers who had already put individual plays out in single quarto editions, and of putting together the whole syndicate of publishers which would be needed to finance the expensive and risky venture of producing such a grand and handsome book. Burbage, sadly, died in 1619 and never lived to see its completion, and at times Heminges and Condell probably doubted whether they ever would either. But the book was at last advertised at the Frankfurt Book Fair in 1622, and, a further year late, it finally appeared in 1623.

Its official title is *Mr William Shakespeares Comedies, Histories, & Tragedies*, but it is now more commonly known simply as the First Folio. Of the 36 plays it includes, 18 had never been printed before, and might have been lost forever had it not been for Heminges and Condell's determination to honour their dead friend: without it the world might not have *Macbeth, Twelfth Night, Julius Caesar* or *The Tempest*, among others. But they wanted to share their pleasure in Shakespeare's work, and in a touching preface addressed 'To the Great Variety of Readers,' they urge us to continue to do so. 'Read him, therefore,' they conclude,

> *and again, and again: And if then you do not like him, surely you are in some manifest danger, not to understand him. And so we leave you to other of his friends, whom if you need, can be your guides:*

*if you need them not, you can lead yourselves,
and others, and such readers we wish him.*

In other words, these plays are so good that only someone who doesn't understand them can fail to enjoy them, but don't worry, there are plenty of people who love Shakespeare already who can help you to do so. And if you love these plays already, you should be ready to share your delight in them with others in your turn.

This book, *For the Love of Shakespeare*, then, offers a snapshot of how the ripples from the splash made in world culture by Heminges and Condell's act of friendship four centuries ago are continuing to spread ever outwards. As well as giving us her own insights into Shakespeare's works, Beth Miller has invited a wide selection of people to share something of their pleasure in Shakespeare, and here are some of their experiences and preferences and observations. As these testimonies make clear once more, we owe a great debt to Shakespeare, and we owe a great debt too to the friends who compiled and published the First Folio. Its contents are extraordinarily good, the source of endless pleasure and insight and stimulation and empathy and laughter and tears. Via Heminge and Condell, this body of drama is our greatest playwright's greatest posthumous bequest. For the love of Shakespeare, keep passing it on.

# INTRODUCTION

## ONE GIANT LEAP

The lights went down, and next to me, my mate Bonny shifted restlessly in her seat. We were seventeen years old, and had been dragged to London on a college trip to see the Shakespeare play we were studying for A level. A hunched figure at the back of the stage leaned heavily on crutches, and I wondered idly how long it was till the interval. Bonny yawned.

Then the figure began reciting those well-known, even hackneyed words, and a shiver went down my spine. 'Now is the winter of our discontent / Made glorious summer by this son of York.'

I barely had time to think, *Gosh, the way he says that makes me wonder what those words mean for the first time ever*, when, in one almighty movement, propelled by his crutches, Richard III leapt right across the enormous stage from one side to the other. It was as if he was flying. All Richard's pent-up rage, his years of being badly treated, his resentments and his hate: they were all there in that one immense, athletic outburst, writ large enough for even a disaffected teenager to see.

Bonny sat up straight, and whispered, 'Bloody hell.'

We both craned forward, elbows on the handrail in front of us, and fell silently, hopelessly in love with Shakespeare.

## TOO HOT, TOO COLD AND JUST RIGHT

Most people who love Shakespeare have a 'switch-on' moment, when he suddenly speaks to them and they finally understand what everyone has been banging on about. When they realise exactly what it means when his work is described as timeless, that the emotions – love, jealousy, lust, ambition – and the relationships Shakespeare explored are as resonant now as they were when the First Folio of his plays was put together.

Some people get Shakespeare right away, from their very first exposure. Others take longer. One of my earliest childhood memories is of being taken to a production of *A Midsummer Night's Dream* at St David's Bishop's Palace in Wales while on our summer holiday. I have a dim memory of seeing actors flit behind the ruined facade of the palace, but the only thing that has stayed with me is the soup I drank during an interval, from a cup – very novel. There were other false starts: reading the plays at school, woodenly, sitting behind desks. Laughing at Bottom's name. OK, that is still funny. A school trip to see a sappy production of *Romeo and Juliet*, at which even our teacher winced during the romantic bits.

It wasn't till I was almost an adult, and saw Antony Sher flinging himself around the stage as Richard III, that I got it. But then I made up for lost time.

I saw Stephen Dillane and Gina Bellman in *Hamlet* in 1994 (though my main memory of that is how hot the Gielgud Theatre was – we all took our shoes and socks off); Haydn Gwynne and Derek Griffiths in *Twelfth Night*, also in 1994 (terrific); Timothy West as Lear in 2003 (gruelling);

*Julius Caesar* performed on the battlements of Conwy Castle (exciting but cold). I saw Simon Russell Beale as Ariel in Sam Mendes' Stratford production of *The Tempest*; this had real magic on stage and was utterly engaging, and just as well, because I was too cheap to pay for a seat and was standing at the back for a fiver. In 1995 I saw Josie Lawrence in *The Taming of the Shrew*, though my husband reminds me that we hated it so much we left in the interval (no offence to Josie – she was very good – but the production was riddled with the difficult-for-modern-audiences-to-swallow sexism of that particular play). There was Ralph Fiennes in *Coriolanus* in 2000 (played in the style of Leonard Rossiter in *Rising Damp* – very odd); and a memorable *Merry Wives of Windsor* in which all the players, including the women, wore stick-on beards that were sent horizontal by a ferocious wind. I've watched a lot of outdoor Shakespeare plays in British summers (bring a blanket, umbrella and flask). And I've seen experimental versions too, such as dreamthinkspeak's *The Rest Is Silence*, a deconstructed *Hamlet* in which the world's most famous soliloquy was said over and over again.

My theatre-going tailed off after having children, but we've taken the kids to see an abridged *Comedy of Errors*, and my daughter trod the boards as Moonshine in *A Midsummer Night's Dream* – ah, I was proud. The children love the Shakespeare song on *Horrible Histories*, which celebrates his unsurpassed facility with words. You haven't seen it? Quickly, rush off and YouTube it now. Good, wasn't it? 'Doo-be-doo-be-doo-be / To be or not to be...' Genius.

And there are some wonderful Shakespeare films: Kenneth Branagh's *Much Ado About Nothing*, and his *Henry V* that convinced despite the tiny cast; *Twelfth Night* with Imogen Stubbs; Claire Danes and Leo DiCaprio in *Romeo + Juliet*...

## THE GAPS

There are plenty of plays I'd never seen or read, till writing this book inspired me to check them out: *Cymbeline*, *Pericles* and *Timon of Athens*, and quite a few of the histories. And as for the poems? Until I began researching this book, I didn't know much about them, apart from 'Shall I compare thee to a summer's day?' (Not the whole poem, just that one line.)

If we're honest, most of us don't know much about Shakespeare. A straw poll of my friends and family revealed the following nuggets, and not much more:

1. He was born and died on the same date. (It turns out this might not be true.)

2. He married Anne Hathaway. (Possibly because she had a cottage?)

3. He lived in Stratford-upon-Avon and London. (There is uncertainty about his commute between the two, given that he probably didn't have a car.)

4. He had a sister. (Most people based this on the fact that there's a band called Shakespears Sister.)

5. He was balding, with a neat beard. Probably not as dishy as Joseph Fiennes in *Shakespeare in Love*. (Actually, we're not really sure what he looked like.)

Writing this book helped me fill a lot of gaps. I hope reading it does the same for you.

## BUT SOFT! ANOTHER SHAKESPEARE BOOK?

Shakespeare's output was staggering. He wrote a shade under 160 poems and 39 plays (or 38 or 40…), of which there have been many thousands of versions and millions of interpretations. Then there are all the controversies, and commentaries, and debates… Amazon lists more than 75,000 books about Shakespeare, excluding his own. The Modern Library has a website which thoughtfully gathers together the 100 best books on Shakespeare, then airily adds at the end of the exhaustive-looking list, 'There are hundreds more fine books on Shakespeare.' Books about the man and his works range from weighty biographies to whimsies such as *Shakespeare's Guide to Parenting*, with every possible stopping point between.

You may wonder, therefore, whether the world needs another book on Shakespeare, but in this year of the 400th anniversary of his death it was too good an opportunity to miss. And it's been a personal voyage of discovery – and rediscovery – that I've enjoyed hugely. So it's a reference book, and it will give an insight into the life and the work, but it's also personal. The book can be read straight through, though it's also designed to be dipped into. My hope is that if you think, *Hey, what's that play where a bear randomly appears?*, then you can flick through Chapter Three and say, 'Of course! It was *The Winter's Tale.*' And if you're trying to decide what Shakespeare film to rent, you can rummage around in Chapter Eight and cry, 'Aha! It's got to be Fassbender's *Macbeth*!'

We are still fascinated by Shakespeare, even after all these centuries of performances and analyses. And that is, of course, because of the writing he gave us. What writing! What words! More than 800,000 of them, spread across an eye-poppingly diverse range of plays and poetry: funny, sad, truthful, informative, groundbreaking words. Words he invented, and phrases we now know as clichés, so embedded are they in our vocabularies. Words he wove together, creating beautiful images, stories that move us and make us laugh, telling universal truths about the human condition; words that bring to life complex, fascinating, rounded characters who we relate to as if they were written yesterday. His influence is felt in art, culture, language, psychology, music…

One of my favourite parts of writing the book was the chance to ask people about *their* Shakespeare: to describe their switch-on moment, discuss their most-loved play and reveal the character they would most like to meet. I interviewed people who are connected to his work in some way: actors, professors, writers, set designers, costumiers, librarians and more. They give details of shivery first performances and describe how they melt into the beauty of his language. They don't hold back on telling us about some duds as well. The interviews are scattered through the book like Ophelia's flowers.

At the time of writing, Shakespeare died 400 years ago, and he looks set for at least another 400 years of analysis, performance, worship, argument and love. His work can be constantly reinvented and tells us things we didn't know about ourselves. I hope it leads you to your own switch-on moment, if you haven't fallen in love with his works yet, or reminds you of your own favourites and guides you to new discoveries. So, at the risk of being spotted with a misquote on my lips, 'Lead on, Macduff'!

Beth Miller
June 2016

# CHAPTER ONE
# SHAKESPEARE THE MAN

## PART ONE
## MAN OF MYSTERY

*The best known and least known of figures.*
**BILL BRYSON**

William Shakespeare, who made far and away the greatest contribution to English literature and language there has ever been, is one of the most infuriatingly mysterious people in history. We don't know very much about him at all. He's not unusual in that; we don't know very much about anyone else who lived four-hundred-and-something years ago either, not even other celebrated writers like Christopher Marlowe and Ben Jonson. The lack of concrete information about Shakespeare has not stopped people speculating, however. Wherever there is a gap, thousands have rushed in to fill it. Shakespeare was a secret Catholic! Shakespeare was gay! The writing of this enigmatic, shadowy figure holds an extraordinary power over us so, naturally, we're keen to know what he was like.

## WE KNOW THEE NOT, OLD MAN

The words of eighteenth-century writer George Steevens still hold remarkably true today:

> *All that is known with any degree of certainty concerning Shakespeare, is – that he was born at Stratford upon Avon, – married and had children there, – went to London, where he commenced actor, and wrote poems and plays, – returned to Stratford, made his will, died, and was buried.*

We do have a bit more detail than that, though much of it is conjecture. There exist about a hundred documents relating to Shakespeare and his family: birth certificates, wills, court records and so on. Other than these dry papers, which give the sketchiest information, and a small batch of eye-witness accounts, all we have are his plays and poetry. We don't have anything which gives us certain access to his innermost thoughts: no diary, no interviews. The first person to try to describe Shakespeare was Nicholas Rowe in 1709, almost 100 years after his death – and of course, Rowe never met him.

To say anything about what Shakespeare the man was like, we have to assume we can tell things about his personality and beliefs from his writing. People have dedicated their lives to reading between the lines. Many have let their imaginations run wild. Maybe we can decipher the man from the page. But more likely we can't, as a quick glance at the huge chasm between the words and lives of most fiction writers will show. Storytellers make a lot of it up and spend a good deal of time *imagining* what things may have been like. The bottom line is, we don't know what Shakespeare was like as a person, only as a writer.

## WHAT DON'T WE KNOW?

❖ The actual dates of his birth and death

❖ What he died of

❖ Anything about his childhood

❖ Exactly how many plays he wrote, nor the order he wrote them in

❖ Whether he attended university

❖ His religion

❖ Whether his marriage was happy

❖ Whether he travelled beyond England

❖ A ton of other things we take for granted that we know about modern-day authors: which writers he most admired, his first kiss, his sources of inspiration, his favourite place to write, his favourite food, his preferred quill...

## DID YOU KNOW?

Although we don't know exactly when Shakespeare was born or when he died, we can make a sensible guess at his birthdate, taking into account the customs of the time, as we know he was baptised on 26 April 1564. And while the actual date he died was not recorded, we know his funeral was on 25 April 1616. For neatness, and national pride, both his birth and death are celebrated on 23 April, St George's Day.

## KEY DATES

1564 – 23 April (probably) – Shakespeare born
1582 – 28 November – Married Anne Hathaway
1583 – 26 May – First child, Susanna, baptised
1585 – 2 February – Twins Hamnet and Judith baptised
1592 – (probably) – First play produced in London
1596 – 11 August – Hamnet buried, aged eleven
1616 – 23 April (probably) – Shakespeare died

## FAMILY

William Shakespeare was born in Stratford-upon-Avon in 1564, to John and Mary. John Shakespeare, a glove-maker, has sometimes been described as illiterate because he signed his name with a mark, but this was relatively common at the time.

Indeed, it's fairly likely that he could read, for he was quite an important figure in Stratford. He held a number of civic posts and steadily rose to one of the highest positions, high bailiff (like a mayor). William's mother, Mary Arden, was the daughter of a reasonably well-to-do farmer who grew up a short distance outside Stratford, in Wilmcote.

He was the third of their eight children, but their eldest surviving child – the two girls born before him both died as babies. Shakespeare's younger siblings were Joan, Anne, Richard, Gilbert and Edmund. We don't know a massive amount about them. Anne died in childhood, and Richard and Gilbert never married. It's thought that Edmund became an actor, though he died young, before William, at the age of 27. Joan lived the longest and, having married and produced children, has a line of descendants who are still around today.

It's assumed that William attended the local grammar school, Kings New School, where he would have been given an excellent grounding in Latin, Greek and other important subjects. This school was open to any local boy, as long as he could read and write. But records from the time are lost. It's believed that he didn't go to university. As he was already a father at the age of 19, it probably wasn't a priority, and it's possible that university in this era was only an option for single men.

## MARRIAGE AND CHILDREN

Shakespeare married Anne Hathaway in 1582, when he was 18. It's long been a source of fascination that Anne was 26, eight years older than him. Shakespeare must have got his father's permission to marry because he was under the age of consent (21 at the time). An expensive marriage bond was purchased – £40, roughly equivalent in today's money to between £6,000 and

£10,000 – in order to allow just one reading of the banns, rather than the customary three, and get the young couple married off quickly. Presumably this was not unconnected to the fact that Anne gave birth to their daughter Susanna only six months later; though it seems odd as it was apparently not that unusual for an Elizabethan bride to be pregnant at her wedding. Another mystery, I'm afraid.

William and Anne had two more children after Susanna: twins called Hamnet and Judith. Sadly Hamnet died at the age of eleven, though the girls both lived to a reasonable age. Susanna married John Hall, a doctor, and they had one daughter, Elizabeth. Judith married rather late, aged 31, to Thomas Quiney, who was fined a month after their wedding for 'carnal copulation' with another woman. Judith and Thomas went on to have three children, but none of the three had offspring, and neither did Susanna's daughter Elizabeth.

## DID YOU KNOW?

Shakespeare's line stopped with granddaughter Elizabeth in 1670. There are, however, numerous descendants of his sister, Joan.

## SHAKESPEARE THE BUSINESSMAN

Thanks to being a part-owner of the theatre company he wrote for, the King's Men, Shakespeare became rather prosperous. In 1597, he purchased New Place, the second biggest house in Stratford, and from then on was based there, commuting to

London as necessary. At some point in the late 1500s, he began to stockpile grain so he could sell it at a profit when it became scarce, though he was fined for hoarding in 1598 when the country was in the grip of famine. A few years later, he bought a large amount of farmland and another house in Stratford. He was, it seems, an intriguing mix of creative genius and hard-headed businessman.

## SHAKESPEARE'S DEATH AND WILL

Shakespeare made his last will in January 1616, and revised it in March, just weeks before he died, aged 52. He left almost everything to his eldest daughter, Susanna, with bequests to his other daughter Judith, various nephews, grandchildren and friends. The will is unexciting other than the famously puzzling line, 'I give unto my wife my second best bed.' This is the only mention of Anne in the will. It's hotly debated whether this was a romantic gesture (the best bed might have been reserved for guests, so the second-best bed would have been the marital bed, with romantic connotations), or an insult, and thus perhaps they were unhappily married. It's one of the very many things we'll never know for sure, though that doesn't stop people speculating.

## DID YOU KNOW?

There is a curse on Shakespeare's grave, which reads:

*Good friend, for Jesus' sake forebeare*
*To digg the dust enclosed heare;*
*Bleste be the man that spares thes stones,*
*And curst be he that moves my bones.*

## THE SPELLING OF SHAKESPEARE'S NAME

Shakespeare never spelled his name the same way twice. The six signatures we know of contain five different variants of his surname: *Shakp, Shakspe, Shaksper, Shakspere* and *Shakspeare*. Those last two, incidentally, are from the three pages of his will, which he must surely have signed at around the same time.

We know that spelling was a fluid business back then. Even so, it's almost like he was trying to be mysterious. The one spelling he didn't seem to favour, oddly, is the one we all use now, Shakespeare – though that's the spelling on the earliest collection of his plays, the First Folio.

## DID YOU KNOW?

In his day, it's possible that his name was pronounced 'Shack-spear'.

## WHAT DID HE LOOK LIKE?

Dark hair, bald on top, pointy little goatee, white ruff, holding a quill, right? Well, probably… There are numerous portraits that purport to be of our man, but only two which are definitively of him. Mind you, it's not certain how accurate they are.

The portrait we all 'know' as Shakespeare is the copperplate engraving from the First Folio, put together a few years after his death. This portrait by the engraver Martin Droeshout would not have been done from life, but is undoubtedly intended to depict Shakespeare, sitting as it does right below his name. It's a shame, then, that it's not a very good picture, with the head strangely disconnected from the body, as if floating on a magic carpet. Ben Jonson wrote an endorsement of this portrait in verse in the First Folio, saying that the engraver 'hath hit His [Shakespeare's] face' well. This has long been regarded as proof of its accuracy. But it has also been suggested that Jonson dashed off these words before he'd seen the picture (then clutched his brow in embarrassment on seeing it, vowing never again to agree to anything after a few beers).

The other portrayal which is definitely of Shakespeare is the statue which sits above his memorial in Holy Trinity Church, Stratford-upon-Avon. It was created by Gerard Johnson and installed in 1623 and, and by golly, it's an odd-looking thing. Maybe it once looked good, but it was whitewashed in 1793 in a fit of madness, so that subsequent repaintings had to be made without any knowledge of the original markings. Many people have been rude about this sculpture, including Thomas Gainsborough, who called it 'a silly smiling thing', and Mark Twain, who said it had 'the deep, deep, deep, subtle, subtle, subtle, expression of a bladder.' Having seen it myself recently, I can confirm that Shakespeare resembles a slightly astonished bank manager.

Less authenticated but better artworks include the classic Chandos portrait, named after a former owner, the Duke of Chandos. It was the founding portrait of the National Portrait Gallery in 1856, where it hangs still. This is the one we'd prefer to be of Shakespeare; he looks suitably dreamy and artistic, and has a cool earring. The picture of Shakespeare on the cover of this book is based on it. The Chandos portrait is from the right period, so if it *is* of Shakespeare it may have been done from life. But we don't honestly know if it's Shakespeare or not.

In 2009, the Shakespeare Birthplace Trust announced that the Cobbe portrait was a depiction of Shakespeare, painted from life in around 1610. In contrast to other portraits, the Cobbe Shakespeare is youngish and handsome, with considerably more hair on top than usual. Not everyone agrees it is a picture of Shakespeare; art expert Roy Strong described the claim as 'codswallop'. Renowned Shakespeare scholar Stanley Wells acknowledged that there's always reasonable doubt, but felt it was '90 per cent' certain to be of Shakespeare. It hangs at Hatchlands Park, a National Trust property in Surrey.

## THE LOST YEARS

There's so much we don't know about Mr S. that the missing periods have been officially designated 'the lost years'. There are two sets of lost years: early and later.

### The Lost Years – Early
This early period is from 1578, when it's reckoned that he left school, at the age of 14, to 1582, when he married Anne Hathaway in a bit of a hurry, aged 18. We know that in 1576, when William was 12, his father, John, was accused of moneylending, which

was illegal. John abruptly withdrew from his many public roles. At some point after that, William might have been removed from school to help support the family. Speculations include him going into the family glove-making business, or working as a teacher or law clerk. He may also have joined one of the theatre troupes that regularly passed through Stratford in that period.

## The Lost Years – Later

It's this second period that really intrigues scholars: the seven years between 1585, when the twins were born, and 1592, when Shakespeare suddenly emerged as a writer in London. The amount of frenzied speculation about what went on in this period – the greatest of all literary vacuums – would fill a hundred libraries.

Some of the suggestions, unsupported by evidence, are: that Shakespeare had to do a runner from Stratford after being caught poaching deer; that he went to Italy; served as a soldier; went on the *Golden Hind* with Francis Drake; was apprenticed to a butcher; went to Lancashire and became a Catholic.

Whatever happened, it's clear he learned his craft as an actor and writer. It's guessed that at some point in the late 1580s, Shakespeare joined the Pembroke's Men theatre troupe, because they performed some of his plays, including *Henry VI*, *The Comedy of Errors* and *Titus Andronicus*.

## THE 'UPSTART CROW' OF LONDON

The lost years end in 1592 with the first mention in print of Shakespeare as a writer. This appears in the autobiography of playwright Robert Greene, and is surprisingly bitchy: Greene describes an 'upstart crow' who 'supposes he is as well able to bombast out a blank verse as the best of you', and 'is in his own conceit the only Shake-scene in a country'. Dearie me, someone sounds a bit jealous! Clearly Shakespeare had made his mark. After Greene's death that same year, his editor, Henry Chettle, made a public apology to Shakespeare about Greene's comments, indicating that Shakespeare was already held in some regard.

# PART TWO
# SHAKESPEARE THE WRITER

## A PLETHORA OF PLAYWRIGHTS

London in the late 1500s was the perfect time to be a playwright. Theatre was the new thing, and it was huge. Shakespeare and all other writers of the day would have been working fast, and at the top of their game, to provide exciting new plays for an insatiable audience. His peers included Christopher Marlowe, Ben Jonson, Thomas Middleton, John Webster, Thomas Dekker, Thomas Kyd, Francis Beaumont and John Fletcher. His main rival in the early years was Marlowe, but he died in 1593 at the age of 29 in a knife fight (though it's been speculated that he was assassinated).

Shakespeare wrote thirty-something plays in 24 years, though he was not by any means the most prolific; Thomas Dekker wrote 32 plays in three years. Certainly all the playwrights of the day would have been rushing to get their work out, which might explain the errors and hastily papered-over cracks in some of Shakespeare's plots. Really, it's astonishing that such a lot of quality plays emerged.

## THE RULE-BREAKERS

Before Shakespeare's time, classical drama had strict rules. These included the restriction that plays had to take place in one day, in one place, with a single plot. They had to be either comedies or tragedies, so you weren't able, for instance, to have a comic scene in a tragedy. And only three performers were allowed to talk in one scene.

Anyone with a passing knowledge of Shakespeare will realise that he broke all these rules, seemingly with happy abandon. His particular speciality was mixing up comedy with tragedy. Only two of his plays follow even one of the rules, taking place over one day and in one location. Other Elizabethan playwrights also experimented hugely with form and content. It must have been a terrifically liberating time to be a writer.

## HOW MANY PLAYS DID HE WRITE?

We don't know exactly. The First Folio contained 36, but it's now accepted that there were a couple more, and he may have contributed to anything up to 42. There could be many more we've never heard of, and others which are lost. Most current lists cite 39, and include *Pericles*, *The Two Noble Kinsmen* and *Edward III*, though it's still a matter of debate as to how involved he was with the last. Several of Shakespeare's plays – mostly later ones – are thought to have been collaborations with other writers. Other more expansive lists include *Double Falsehood* and *Sir Thomas More*.

For the purposes of this book I've gone with the classic 39. Each play has its own entry, other than some of the history plays, which make more sense cosied up together. The plays are segregated by the classic though often unhelpful categorisation that has been in place since the First Folio: Comedies, Histories and Tragedies. Many *Complete Works* nowadays don't divide the works up in this way (including *The Oxford*, which lists them chronologically, and *The Arden*, which lists them alphabetically). This makes sense, because so many plays are hard to classify. However, I've gone for it anyway, sticking to alphabetical order within the comedies and tragedies, and chronological with the histories.

## WHAT ORDER WERE THE PLAYS WRITTEN IN?

You may not be surprised to hear that we don't know for sure. No two lists are in the same order. We don't even know which play he wrote first; depending on which scholar you believe, it might have been *The Two Gentlemen of Verona*, *The Taming of the Shrew*, *Titus Andronicus*, *The Comedy of Errors* or one of the *Henry VI*s. All we really have to go on are theories about the relative maturity of the style of writing, dates before which they could not have been written because of events they allude to, or dates after which they couldn't have been written because of when they were first performed.

## TURNING BASE METAL INTO GOLD

Many of Shakespeare's plays were based on earlier works by other authors. He borrowed plots and characters, sometimes even whole lines. This was not for a minute regarded as plagiarism in the way that we might consider it now. Elizabethans valued the retelling of familiar stories in new ways, and reinventing the familiar was something Shakespeare excelled at. He repeatedly reworked the plot of a pedestrian text, changing characters or adding new ones, producing something extraordinary and distinct. Only a couple of plays – *Love's Labour's Lost* and *The Tempest* – appear not to be based on an earlier story.

Even George Bernard Shaw, who wasn't exactly a fan ('It would positively be a relief to me to dig him up and throw stones at him'), acknowledged, albeit reluctantly, that Shakespeare had 'enormous power over language' and was a master of the art of reinventing a story, 'provided someone else told it to him first'.

## THE FIRST FOLIO

Seven years after Shakespeare's death, two actors in his theatrical company, John Heminges and Henry Condell, published a book called *Mr. William Shakespeares Comedies, Histories, & Tragedies*. This book, always referred to as the First Folio, contains 36 of his plays. Without their work, it's likely that at least half, if not all, the plays would have been lost. Before the First Folio, the only printed copies of Shakespeare's plays were in cheap, low-quality editions called quartos, and just 17 or 18 plays appear to have been published in this format.

Because Heminges and Condell had worked alongside Shakespeare, they knew his work as well as anyone. They compiled versions of the plays from quarto copies, as well as from rough drafts written by Shakespeare and the copies used by the company to perform the plays. Two hundred and thirty-three copies of the First Folio are known to exist (roughly 750 copies were printed). The largest collection of 82 copies is in Washington, D.C. at the Folger Shakespeare Library. The British Library owns five, and Oxford's Bodleian Library has put their copy on their website so you can digitally turn the pages of the book.

Unknown copies periodically turn up: one was discovered in France in 2014, in a public library. Copies of the First Folio always feature in lists of the most valuable books in the world. The current record holder is one in New York that sold for $6.16 million (£3.73 million) in 2001.

The First Folio was reprinted three times in the seventeenth century: the Second Folio (1632), Third Folio (1663) and Fourth Folio (1685). The third and fourth added new plays, most of which are no longer believed to have been written by Shakespeare.

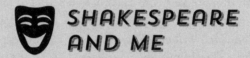

# SHAKESPEARE AND ME

*Kate Pitt has worked at the Folger Shakespeare Library in Washington, D.C. in a variety of positions in Public Programs and as an ambassador for the Shakespeare Society in New York. She studied at RADA (Royal Academy of Dramatic Art) and Shakespeare and Company.*

### What was your switch-on moment?

I saw a beautiful outdoor production of *A Midsummer Night's Dream* at Edith Wharton's Mount when I was little. The mechanicals drove up in a jeep and there were fairies with lights on their heads moving through the woods. It was magical, and later supplemented by an incredible teacher named Jane Mallison who taught my seventh-grade English class. She had us all perform speeches from the play, and I got up there with a broom and a cap as Puck and was hooked.

**Which is your favourite of Shakespeare's plays?**

I often get grabbed by whichever play I've just seen, but *Midsummer*, *Othello* and *Twelfth Night* are constants, with *Antony and Cleopatra*, *Richard II* and *All's Well* as recent additions.

**Tell us about the most memorable performance you've seen.**

I was first introduced to Shakespeare through film so those performances tend to stick with me the most. The 1999 *Midsummer* film with Kevin Kline is pure joy and the Branagh *Much Ado* and *Henry V* were favourite films as a kid. The long tracking shot during the 'Non Nobis' where you get a glimpse of all the characters in the aftermath of Agincourt – Exeter stomping through with his mace, a silent Montjoy watching the King carry the boy off the field – is so viscerally powerful when added to all the incredible language that has come before it. And to follow the battle with the pure delight of the Kate-wooing and the black-coated Chorus closing the door – all powerfully memorable moments.

**Which Shakespeare character would you most like to meet?**

Queen Margaret.

> **How would you persuade somebody to give Shakespeare a chance?**
>
> I would ask them to see a great production or film and hope that they would be moved, entertained, or changed in some way by seeing a piece of themselves or their lives on stage.

## THE POETRY

Shakespeare is as celebrated for his 154 sonnets (short poems) as his plays. They contain some of his most famous lines – 'Rough winds do shake the darling buds of May', for instance. He also wrote four long poems: *Venus and Adonis*, *The Rape of Lucrece*, *A Lover's Complaint* and *The Phoenix and the Turtle*. The poems have their own separate chapter.

## SHAKESPEARE AS ACTOR

We don't know when Shakespeare first started acting, but by 1594 he was a member of a theatrical troupe, the Lord Chamberlain's Men, later the King's Men, and he stayed with them for the rest of his working life. Shakespeare acted throughout his writing career, and most likely directed his own plays as well, which must have been a tricky juggling act. It's probable he only took on small parts in his own plays – the Ghost in *Hamlet* is popularly associated with him – but he took on larger parts for other playwrights. For example, in 1598 he took a principal role in Ben Jonson's *Every Man in His Humour*.

## THE AUTHORSHIP CONTROVERSY

Some people wouldn't attribute *any* plays to Shakespeare because they believe the works associated with him were written by someone else. There are some very solid and obvious reasons why these theories don't hold water; in fact, it's pretty clear that Shakespeare was indeed the author of the plays that bear his name. I'll discuss the so-called 'authorship question' in more detail in the Chapter Eight.

## CHAPTER TWO
# SHAKESPEARE'S WORLD

## PART ONE
# ENGLAND, STRATFORD AND LONDON

### THIS BLESSED PLOT, THIS EARTH, THIS REALM, THIS ENGLAND

When Shakespeare was born, Queen Elizabeth I had been on the throne for six years. But uneasy was the head that wore the crown and plots (real and imagined) to unseat her were everywhere. Times were tense, and the court were always on their guard for potential assassination attempts. Who would succeed Elizabeth, and the impact that would have on the country, was a massive concern throughout her reign. It's probably not a coincidence that so many of Shakespeare's plays – about a quarter of them – focus on the issue of royal succession. It would have been a topic on everyone's mind.

These were tense times in terms of religion too. This was the period after the Reformation, when it wasn't certain whether England would return to the Roman faith or not. People looked to Elizabeth to consolidate the Reformation and Protestantism. Under her rule, Catholics weren't allowed to practise their faith publicly, though they could opt out of attending Protestant services by paying a small sum as a 'recusant' (refuser). When this fine was later abruptly increased, most recusants capitulated and, outwardly at least, adopted Protestantism.

On top of all this, the sixteenth century was not a healthy time to be born into. Horrible diseases were rife: TB, scurvy, dysentery, smallpox and the ever-present terror of plague. People tended to have large families so that at least some of their children made it to adulthood. Life expectancy was not much more than 40; in some places, much lower.

## STRATFORD-UPON-AVON

When Shakespeare was born there, Stratford was, by the standards of the time, a substantial and busy place. Its population of 2,000 may sound small to us, but at the time there were only three cities in the UK with populations greater than 10,000. For comparison, there are now more than 70 towns and cities in the UK with populations greater than 100,000. It's statistics like this that make you realise why the post office queue is always so long.

But if Stratford seemed big then, it must have blown Shakespeare's mind when he first went to London and found that a single theatre there held as many people, if not more, than his entire home town (audience capacity at some theatres is estimated to have been between 1,500 and 3,000).

Stratford was roughly a four-day walk from London, or a two-day horse ride, part of a well-established route between the capital and Wales used for the transfer of wool. It was also a regular port of call for troupes of touring actors, so the young Shakespeare would probably have seen plenty of plays, particularly since his father, as bailiff, had to distribute the licences which permitted performances.

## DID YOU KNOW?

You can visit several properties connected to Shakespeare in Stratford, including his birthplace in Henley Street. But you can't see New Place, the house Shakespeare bought once he'd made some money, because a subsequent owner, Reverend Francis Gastrell, pulled it down in 1759, apparently after losing patience with rubbernecking Shakespeare fans peeking through the windows! You can visit the gardens though, which are owned by the Shakespeare Birthplace Trust.

## SHAKESPEARE'S LONDON

We don't have detailed records of London in Shakespeare's time. We can be sure, though, that it was nothing like today's sprawling metropolis. The London he lived in was still a town, with a population of around 150,000. This much smaller city covered a similar area to that which is now called the City of London (not to be confused with the much bigger, lower-case city of London), and was bordered by city walls. But it was still the bustling centre of government, trade and culture. In Europe, only Paris and Naples were larger. To make his name, London was where Shakespeare had to be.

The first things that would have hit the slightly sheltered twenty-something from Stratford would have been the noise and the smell. The streets of late 1580s London were narrow and crowded, with houses jutting out across the streets, almost touching each other. He would have heard the cries of street traders, the sound of horses' hooves striking stone and the shouts of brawling drinkers outside the many taverns. Water was too dirty to drink, and tea and coffee had yet to arrive, so people drank beer, or wine if they could afford it. In addition to Londoners' rare sobriety, talk had to be loud to be heard above the general hubbub. It's a miracle Shakespeare found anywhere quiet enough to sit down and write.

The crowded streets must have stunk of unwashed bodies, sweat and rotting refuse. As there was no supply of clean water, people would go for weeks without washing. The rats, which lived off the rubbish in the streets, hosted the fleas which carried the bubonic plague.

Death and disease were everywhere and inescapable, especially for the poor. Criminals were still hanged in public, and the severed heads of executed lawbreakers were displayed at the Southwark end of London Bridge at Traitors' Gate (eateries, cycle shops and office blocks characterise the area today).

There were no flushing toilets so human waste and rubbish were thrown into the Thames, or simply dumped in the street. The Thames was also the main way people and goods were moved from one place to another, on the many boats. The only way across the river other than by boat was London Bridge, full to bursting with shops, merchants, people, and heads on spikes; one of the busiest places in an already crazy-busy town.

Staple Inn in Holborn, although damaged in the Blitz, gives a sense of what houses of the time would have looked like: two or three storeys, and a bit higgledy-piggledy. By far the tallest building, with a spire of 140 metres, was the old St Paul's Cathedral, later destroyed in the Great Fire of 1666. This was larger than the Christopher-Wren-designed St Paul's that replaced it, but would be dwarfed in today's London by the Shard at 309 metres. St Paul's was a social as well as religious centre, with the central nave filled with people selling ale, bread and fruit. Shakespeare might have known it, as it was where booksellers were located. Close to the cathedral was the Mermaid Tavern, which legend (though not most scholars) claims is where Shakespeare drank and bantered with fellow playwright Ben Jonson.

The Tower of London and Southwark Cathedral (formerly St Mary Overie) are amongst the few things in modern London that Shakespeare would still be able to recognise. Though he would probably be amazed to see the Globe, the theatre in which some of his most famous plays were first performed, resurrected and flourishing again.

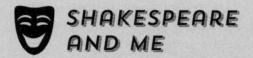

## SHAKESPEARE AND ME

*Clive Depper is Visitor Engagement Manager at the Shakespeare Birthplace Trust. His main responsibility is training the guides and the four actors who form the in-house troupe, Shakespeare Aloud!*

**Which is your favourite Shakespeare play?**
Really difficult to pick one, but a good production of *Henry IV, Part I* takes some beating.

**What's the most memorable performance you've seen?**
I've been so fortunate to see many memorable performances, but if I had to pick one it would be David Warner as Hamlet at the RSC (Royal Shakespeare Company) in 1966. I was 18, I had slept out to get a standing-only ticket and I can still recall vividly his performance. It was a Hamlet for my generation, with his long red scarf and long grey coat – very much the student uniform of the day. When he spoke the verse, it was far more conversational and, to my ears, realistic than the often declamatory way that was still favoured by many classically trained actors of the day.

**Which Shakespeare character would you most like to meet?**
Iago in *Othello*, Rosalind and Jaques in *As You Like It*. It would also be enjoyable to have a pint or two with Falstaff and his cronies, and I know who would be paying!

**How would you persuade somebody to give Shakespeare a chance?**
I have always believed that the plays were written to be performed, as long as they are done well. Any

of Shakespeare's plays can work their magic, but *Richard III*, *Twelfth Night* or *Macbeth* I would highly recommend. They will transport you to another time and place where you can experience life lived to the full by humans many centuries ago, but which has a stinging relevance for us today.

# PART TWO
# THEATRE IN SHAKESPEARE'S DAY

## THEATRE AS MASS ENTERTAINMENT

During Shakespeare's writing life, theatre was an astonishingly popular form of entertainment, with hundreds, sometimes thousands, of people going to see plays every day. Audiences would expect a constantly updated programme of plays, rather like cinemagoers expect now. Most companies performed five, maybe even six, plays in a week.

The design of these early theatres grew from the way plays were staged in medieval England, when there were no permanent theatres, and morality plays were performed by travelling players in the yards of galleried inns. The George in Southwark, now owned by the National Trust, is the only surviving inn of this type in London. The stage was simply a platform raised at one end of the inn yard. The 'groundlings' would have stood in the yard, while wealthier patrons watched from the galleries above.

The first successful London theatre, imaginatively called the Theatre, opened in 1576 in Shoreditch. It was built by actor-manager James Burbage, and later run by his sons, Cuthbert and Richard (the leading actor in Shakespeare's troupe). It was so popular that a rival, the Curtain, was built close by two years later.

All was well for more than 20 years, and some of Shakespeare's early plays must have been performed here. But then the cost of the land lease was raised to an unacceptable level. The building itself, however, was owned by the Burbage brothers, and an extraordinary plan was hatched. One cold night in December 1598, so the story goes, a team of demolition men dismantled the Theatre stick by stick, and carried its timbers on carts across the frozen Thames to a new site south of the river, in Southwark.

## DID YOU KNOW?

Plays were not permitted to be performed inside the City of London because of fears of the plague spreading amongst tightly packed audiences. Thus all theatres were built outside its walls, in places like Shoreditch and Southwark, where city laws and regulations did not apply.

## THE GLOBE

The new theatre built from the Theatre's timbers opened in 1599. It was called the Globe, and was most likely a polygonal building, probably with about 20 sides, not far off the 'wooden O' mentioned in the prologue of *Henry V*. An 'apron' stage jutted out into the audience, within spitting distance – literally – of the actors. The Globe was just a few yards away from a rival playhouse, the Rose, which had opened 12 years earlier, meaning that this seamy area of Southwark, home to taverns and brothels, became the centre of London theatre.

Audiences, the majority of whom would come from the City across the river, were alerted to new plays by means of a large banner on a flagpole and by fanfares. Plays were always put on at two o'clock, and the Globe could accommodate something in the region of 3,000 people. Groundling tickets were cheap: a penny (the cost of a loaf of bread). For two pence you could watch from the relative comfort of the gallery.

It was probably at the Globe where the fruits of Shakespeare's most astonishingly creative period were performed: *Hamlet*, *Romeo and Juliet*, *King Lear*, *Othello* and *Macbeth*, amongst others.

In 1613, during a performance of *Henry VIII*, a rogue spark from a stage cannon ignited the thatched roof, and the Globe burned down, luckily with no fatalities. It was quickly rebuilt the following year, this time with a tiled roof, though today's reconstructed Globe has gone back to thatch (decorated with discreet and very twenty-first-century sprinklers).

## DID YOU KNOW?

Today's Globe Theatre, which stands on London's Bankside, is about 230 metres away from the first Globe's location. It's not based on the original Globe (for beyond the thatched roof we have no record of what that was like), but instead was designed using drawings of another theatre of the time, the Swan, made in 1596 by a Dutch tourist.

## AUDIENCES AND ON-STAGE ACTION

The audience would have been much less respectful than theatre-goers today, even without mobile phones going off, and there was plenty of 'audience participation'. Groundlings, close packed and smelling of ale and sweat, booed and even spat at the actors if they didn't like the play. Some sat on the edge of the stage, and there are recorded instances of audience members strolling from one side of the stage to the other, heedless of the action being played out.

Playgoers would not have expected, nor got, much in the way of scenery, and there were no curtains, not even at the theatre called the Curtain. There were lavish costumes, though, and gruesome special effects in battle scenes – courtesy of animal organs and blood. In Shakespeare's day, women were not allowed on stage, and young men played female parts. Women did, however, perform on stage in Europe at that time, and in England from 1660 onwards.

## THE LORD CHAMBERLAIN'S MEN

Acting troupes needed to attach themselves to patrons to avoid accusations of homelessness – the vagrancy laws were tough. Luckily, patrons, usually noblemen, were keen on collecting troupes as it was good for prestige. The Lord Chamberlain,

Lord Hunsdon, provided Shakespeare's troupe with money and, just as importantly, respectability. It's thought that Shakespeare joined the group when it was formed in 1594, and stayed with them for the rest of his working life. When Queen Elizabeth died, King James I took on the patronage of the troupe and thereafter they were known, naturally, as the King's Men.

The Chamberlain's Men was made up of a group of eight 'sharers', who owned the Globe and split profits and debts. There would also have been other actors and workers associated with the troupe who weren't owners. The sharers included Shakespeare; Richard Burbage, the leading actor; Will Kemp, who took most of the comic roles; and John Heminges and Henry Condell, who later edited the First Folio. This was the main way Shakespeare made his money. Playwriting was not then (indeed, it still isn't) a lucrative profession. Shakespeare's contemporaries Ben Jonson and Thomas Dekker both died in poverty (despite Jonson's popularity and Dekker's prolific output).

There were other acting troupes, but many disbanded during the 'plague years', when theatres were closed to stem the spread of disease, and companies had to go on tour. By the late 1590s, the only real rivals to the Chamberlain's Men were the Admiral's Men, led by actor Edward Alleyn and impresario Philip Henslowe, based a stone's throw away at the Rose.

## DID YOU KNOW?

The Chamberlain's Men were inadvertently pulled into a royal scandal in 1601, when the Earl of Essex commissioned a performance of *Richard II*. This was controversial as it dealt with the overthrow of a king, and Essex's desire to overthrow Elizabeth I was known. He was later executed. Shakespeare and Co. must have feared for their lives, but luckily the Queen was forgiving and accepted their explanation that they'd done it for the money, not rebellion.

## THE BLACKFRIARS THEATRE

The Globe was an open-air theatre – the roof only covered the stage and gallery – so could only be used in the summer months. The King's Men really hit the big time when they took over the Blackfriars Theatre north of the river in 1608. The Blackfriars had a full roof and artificial lighting for winter performances. It also allowed musical accompaniment, which might be the reason why some of Shakespeare's later plays (*Cymbeline*, *The Winter's Tale*, *The Tempest*) feature singing. Though it seated fewer people than the Globe, and the entrance price was higher, the Blackfriars soon became the main theatre in London. It was the prototype for the kind of theatres we would recognise today. The Sam Wanamaker Playhouse, next door to the Globe, is a partial reconstruction of the Blackfriars.

## DID YOU KNOW?

Dividing a play into acts is believed to have started at the Blackfriars Theatre. Being indoors, it used candles for lighting. These couldn't last for the full length of a play, so act divisions were introduced, allowing the candles to be replaced.

## BOOM AND BUST

Southwark was soon a booming theatre district, with the Rose, the Globe, the Swan and later the Hope. For a time, the authorities were all in favour of theatre. Queen Elizabeth I was keen on the entertainment, and presumably pretty keen too on the money her government earned from theatre licences. When King James I took the throne in 1603, he also supported the performing arts. But there was a groundswell of dissent from the Puritans, a group of Protestants who regarded theatres as dens of immorality. (Actually, they may have been right about that.) They succeeded in closing the theatres down in 1642, and the Globe was demolished two years later. Though the remaining theatres were reopened by Charles II in 1660, they were never again to be the huge places of mass entertainment that they were in Shakespeare's era.

## CHAPTER THREE
# THE COMEDIES

Generally the comedies are characterised by witty wordplay, a convoluted plot, a sense of fun, even daftness, and no deaths. Some of them are amongst the most popular plays ever written. However, there are several which don't fit comfortably into the 'comedy' category and a handful have long been classed as 'problem plays': *All's Well That Ends Well*, *Measure for Measure* and *The Merchant of Venice*, which all have a certain dark ambiguity that leaves the playgoer scratching their head and muttering, 'OK, Will, I'll take your word for it that this is a *comedy…*'

Others have themes which aren't particularly funny, though in the hands of the right director and actors they can be: *The Taming of the Shrew*, for instance (violence towards a woman), or *The Winter's Tale* (destructive jealousy). Some are dreamlike and psychological rather than comedic (*The Tempest*), while others feature unfunny deaths (*The Two Noble Kinsmen*, *The Winter's Tale*). Nearly all the comedies have a serious thread running through them.

# ALL'S WELL THAT ENDS WELL

*All's Well* is one of the so-called problem plays. There's certainly enough underlying darkness and ambiguity here to make us feel quite uncomfortable.

## PLOT

The King of France is very ill, and sends for his ward, a handsome chap named Bertram, to comfort him in his last hours. Bertram sets off, leaving behind his recently widowed mother, the Countess of Roussillon, and her servant, Helen (sometimes known as Helena). Helen is in mourning too as her father, the court physician, has just died. However, the Countess suspects correctly that Helen is also sad because she's secretly in love with Bertram. The Countess gives Helen her blessing, and sends her off to the King to offer her medical skills (and perhaps snag Bertram while she's at it).

The King conveniently says that if Helen cures him, he'll give her the hand of any young swain she fancies. Having inherited her father's medical gifts, Helen does indeed heal the King and, of course, chooses Bertram. This young man is extremely reluctant, as she's only a doctor's daughter. And, presumably, because he doesn't love her. Anyway, Bertram has to go through with it because the King orders him to, but he immediately tells his new bride that he'll never really be her husband unless she has the family ring from his finger, and gets pregnant by him. To avoid the possibility of either of these things happening, he immediately rushes off to fight in Italy.

Helen disconsolately follows him, disguised as a pilgrim. She finds he's planning to bed a virgin named Diana. Helen and Diana cook up a plot in which Diana agrees to sleep with Bertram if he swaps his ring for hers (it's actually one of Helen's). At the last minute Diana and Helen change places, and thus Helen consummates her marriage without the groom knowing. This scene happens, coyly, off stage. We must assume it's very dark for Bertram not to notice the substitution, unless we want to imply that men cannot tell one lass from another.

Helen starts rumours that she has died, and returns to France. She plans to tell the King what's happened, but it looks like it might be too late for, believing she's dead, an old friend of the Countess has offered *his* daughter to marry Bertram. That Bertram sure is catnip to the ladies. The King, noticing that the ring Bertram offers as an engagement ring belongs to Helen, thinks Bertram has murdered her. But, in the nick of time, in comes Diana with Bertram's ring, accompanied by a pregnant Helen, to prove that Bertram's marriage stipulations have been met. Now Bertram has to settle down with Helen, though it does beg the question: why does she still want him?

## IN A NUTSHELL

Girl tricks a chap into marrying her.

## OTHER NOTABLE CHARACTERS

Paroles, an unpopular chum of Bertram's. He's tricked into bad-mouthing his fellow soldiers, and is roundly humiliated.

## BODY COUNT

None during the play, apart from Helen's fake death. The Countess's husband and Helen's father have died shortly before, and the King is on his last legs. Indeed, the entire older generation speak repeatedly of their feebleness and/or encroaching deaths, casting rather a pall over a supposed comedy.

## DID YOU KNOW?

❖ This play isn't often performed, perhaps because it has a reputation as unlucky – early performances were dogged by actors' illnesses.

❖ Some people speculate that *All's Well* is the lost play *Love's Labour's Won*. But most think it was written too late for that, around 1605.

❖ Both this play and *Cymbeline* were likely to have been based on the fourteenth-century *Decameron*, a collection of stories by Boccaccio.

 QUOTABLE LINES

*'Our remedies oft in ourselves do lie*
*Which we ascribe to heaven.'*

*'Love all, trust a few,*
*Do wrong to none.'*

*'A young man married is a man that's marred.'*

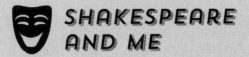

# SHAKESPEARE AND ME

*Madeleine Cox is the Reading Room Services Coordinator at the Shakespeare Birthplace Trust.*

### What was your switch-on moment?

When I came to work here, I'd only read one Shakespeare play (*Romeo and Juliet*) at school, and the only performances I'd seen were on outings when I worked at Marks and Spencer! One key moment in my growing affection for Shakespeare was when a close friend told me the story of *Cymbeline*, a play I didn't know, in such a witty way that I couldn't wait to read it. Another key experience was when I had to learn a Shakespeare speech from *As You Like It* by heart for a theatre evening class. Practising saying the words really gave me a new appreciation of Shakespeare's language.

### Which is your favourite of Shakespeare's plays?

For many years it was *Hamlet*, partly as it contains so many of those famous Shakespeare quotes, and also because of its darker, existential nature. Now I have a soft spot for *Pericles* and *Cymbeline*, and for *Much Ado About Nothing*; I love the characters of Beatrice and Benedick and the happy ending. *Love's Labour's Lost* is a favourite too, as I remember typing up Stanley Wells's notes for the Oxford edition.

**Tell us about the most memorable performance you've seen.**

It was *All's Well That Ends Well* in 2014 at the RSC (Royal Shakespeare Company). The characters seemed completely psychologically believable and I was sucked in from the very start. Some productions leave me looking at my watch and wondering when the interval (with accompanying ice cream!) will arrive, but this production was so gripping I lost all sense of time. I've also really enjoyed watching students on our residential courses perform productions. Last year students from Hanover College performed scenes from *Love's Labour's Lost* in the Birthplace garden which were really inventive and laugh-out-loud funny, and had a really immediate quality that I like to think Shakespeare's original staging might have had, free from the constraints of props and setting.

# AS YOU LIKE IT

*As You Like It* is described as a pastoral comedy, meaning it has a simple countryside setting, involving shepherds and other such bucolic touches. Despite its rather thin plot, *As You Like It* has long been popular because it's a dreamy, light-hearted, love-centred fairy tale. And it has a great female character, the funny and resourceful Rosalind.

## PLOT

Oliver, having inherited his father's estate, is supposed to look after his younger brother, Orlando. But Oliver is a meanie, and won't give his brother any money. When he hears that Orlando plans to take part in a wrestling competition to earn some cash, he encourages the opponent, Charles, a big fella, to pummel him good.

Over at the royal court, Celia and Rosalind are cousins and best friends. But Rosalind is miserable as her father, Duke Senior, has been removed from the throne by his brother (Celia's father), Duke Frederick, and banished to the leafy Forest of Arden. The lasses cheer themselves up by watching the wrestling competition, and when Orlando bravely and unexpectedly defeats Charles, Rosalind falls in love with Orlando (and he with her). Hearing that Oliver is planning to have him killed, Orlando sensibly legs it to the forest and is welcomed into Duke Senior's camp.

Rosalind also heads to the forest as Duke Frederick banishes her along with her father. Celia accompanies her, as does the court jester Touchstone. The women disguise themselves (of course they do – this is Shakespeare) as a young man called Ganymede and his sister Aliena. Celia's departure puts Duke Frederick in a fury. He raises an army to get rid of his annoying forest-based brother and sends Oliver to go and retrieve Celia.

Orlando moons around the forest leaving love poems for Rosalind on trees, as you do. Rosalind, disguised as Ganymede, offers to instruct him in the ways of love, suggesting that Orlando woo him as though he was Rosalind. To confuse matters further, a young woman called Phoebe falls in love with Ganymede, despite having her own lovelorn suitor, Silvius.

When Oliver reaches the forest, he's attacked by a lioness and rescued by Orlando. The two brothers agree to be friends – rather decent of Orlando under the circs. Oliver falls in love with the shepherdess Aliena (aka Celia).

A big wedding day is planned, though it isn't entirely clear who will pair off with who. Rosalind and Celia appear out of disguise, and rope in the god of marriage, Hymen, to marry everyone. Rosalind marries Orlando, Celia marries Oliver, Phoebe marries Silvius (because Ganymede turned out to be a gal), and Touchstone marries Audrey, a goatherd. The news then arrives that Duke Frederick has been convinced to change his ways and return the throne to his brother. It all ends happily, with dancing and plans to return to the royal court.

## IN A NUTSHELL

Rosalind helps everyone find love in the forest and, despite gender confusion, finds it herself too.

## OTHER NOTABLE CHARACTERS

Jaques (pronounced 'Jay-kweez') is one of the lords who lives in the forest with Duke Senior. Often known as 'the melancholy Jaques', he's not essential to the plot but is an observer, philosopher and cynic. He has one of Shakespeare's greatest speeches, 'All the world's a stage...'

## DID YOU KNOW?

❖ *As You Like It* is thought to be the play which opened the new Globe Theatre in 1599.

❖ The complex and compelling Rosalind has more lines than any other female character in Shakespeare, save for Cleopatra.

❖ Adam, Orlando's servant, is a part traditionally believed to have been played by Shakespeare (though there's no hard evidence for this).

❖ *As You Like It* contains more marriages than any other Shakespeare play.

❖ The play is based on a romantic novel of 1590, *Rosalynde*, by Thomas Lodge. This in turn was based on an old poem, 'The Tale of Gamelyn', which was included in Chaucer's *Canterbury Tales* (though not written by Chaucer).

❖ The Forest of Arden might be the Ardennes, in northern France. This would make sense as the rest of the play takes place in France. But it might also be a reference to Arden near Stratford-upon-Avon, an area which contained the village of Wilmcote, where Shakespeare's mother, Mary Arden, came from.

##  QUOTABLE LINES

'The fool doth think he is wise, but the wise man
knows himself to be a fool.'

'All the world's a stage,
And all the men and women merely players.
They have their exits and their entrances,
And one man in his time plays many parts.'

**THIS FAMOUS SPEECH THEN SEGUES INTO
THE SEVEN AGES OF MAN...**

'At first the infant,
Mewling and puking in the nurse's arms.
Then the whining schoolboy with his satchel
And shining morning face, creeping like snail
Unwillingly to school.'

**IT CONTINUES THROUGH THE AGES, UNTIL THE LAST CUTTING
LINE DEPICTING THE FINAL AGE OF MAN:**

'Sans teeth, sans eyes, sans taste, sans everything.'

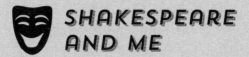

# SHAKESPEARE AND ME

*Professor Michael Dobson is Director of the Shakespeare Institute, Stratford-upon-Avon, and Professor of Shakespeare Studies at the University of Birmingham.*

## What was your switch-on moment?

I'd found the text of *Macbeth* fascinating in a school classroom at 13, but it wasn't until I was taken in a bus to see Terry Hands's RSC production of *Henry V* when I was doing it for O level that it hit me: this amazing, rich poetry actually gets spoken in real time, it is the medium for compelling drama, everyone on stage has a contending, fiercely articulated viewpoint! It was a stunning production and I resolved there and then to see many more.

## Which is your favourite of Shakespeare's plays?

The fact that I have a daughter called Rosalind is perhaps a giveaway: *As You Like It* is at once so slight, so serious, so generous, and I had a lovely time being Amiens the minstrel on an island in Poole Harbour one summer. Adrian Noble's production in 1985, with Alan Rickman as Jaques, continues to haunt my memory, as does Sam West's in 2006. I was a consultant on that one; it was a lovely experience. That play makes such a wonderful use of the provisionality of theatre, it's such a hypothetical play: what if we were in Arcadia, and it was also Warwickshire, and also France, and there was a wicked uncle and a clown and a disdainful shepherdess, and we could try out dressing up and being in love...?

**Tell us about the most memorable performance you've seen.**

Several contenders there! Trevor Nunn's *All's Well That Ends Well*, with Harriet Walter and Peggy Ashcroft – Chekhovian, beautifully observed, detailed, bittersweet, poignant. Lucy Bailey's *A Midsummer Night's Dream*, set in a contemporary, scruffy edge-land in Manchester – funny, ecologically savvy, endlessly inventive. Jan Klata's *Titus Andronicus* in Gdańsk in 2014, with a Polish company playing the Goths in Polish and a German company playing the Romans in German, a stunning piece of traumatic black comedy in exquisitely, violently bad taste.

**Which Shakespeare character would you most like to meet?**

That would depend very much on who was playing her or him at the time! I'm sure I could have spent a long time with Janet Suzman's Cleopatra if I'd ever had the opportunity...

> **How would you persuade somebody to give Shakespeare a chance?**
>
> I'd insist on taking them to a really good live performance. Simple, but the entire point.

# THE COMEDY OF ERRORS

Two sets of twins, with the same names, separated from each other… What can possibly go wrong? Played well, *Errors* has enormous potential for excellent wordplay and slapstick.

## PLOT

The cities of Ephesus and Syracuse are at war, and people who travel between them face the death penalty. That's bad news for the elderly Egeon from Syracuse, who's just turned up in Ephesus, trying to find his missing family. He tells his story to the Duke of Ephesus.

It goes like this. Years ago, Egeon and his wife had twin sons, both called Antipholus (why?!). They also had twin boys for servants, both called Dromio (why again?!). The family was separated by that reliable Shakespearean plot device, a storm at sea. Egeon ended up with one son and one servant, his wife with the other set, and they all lost track of each other. The son that stayed with Egeon, Antipholus of Syracuse (henceforth Antipholus S.) is now an adult, and he and his servant Dromio of Syracuse (Dromio S.) had set off to find their brothers, but never returned.

Now Egeon has come to look for his son in Ephesus. The sympathetic Duke agrees to delay his execution.

By staggering coincidence, Antipholus S. turns up in Ephesus that very day. He sends Dromio S. off on an errand, and is baffled when the identical Dromio of Ephesus (Dromio E.) turns up, denying all knowledge of the errand and, furthermore, saying that his wife wants him to come to dinner. Not having a wife, Antipholus S. assumes it's a rotten joke and wallops the baffled Dromio E., who then returns to Adriana, the wife of Antipholus E. He tells her that her 'husband' claims not to know her. With me so far?

When Dromio S. returns from the errand, he naturally knows nothing about some joke he's meant to have made about a non-existent wife. Antipholus S. begins beating *him* now. Then Adriana shows up and insists that Antipholus S. comes back with her. Confused, Antipholus S. does so, meaning that when her actual husband, Antipholus E., returns, he's forbidden entry to his own house.

Antipholus S. falls in love with Adriana's sister, Luciana, who's shocked by her brother-in-law's behaviour. Dromio S. meanwhile discovers that he's apparently engaged to a kitchen maid, who's 'spherical, like a globe'. Much confusion ensues, with accusations of infidelity, arrests, concealment in a priory and non-payment for a gold chain. All is finally resolved by both sets of twins arriving in the same place at the same time. The priory's Abbess, Emilia, reveals herself to be Egeon's long-lost wife. Everyone is variously reunited, pardoned, and in Antipholus S.'s case, able to woo Luciana with a clear conscience.

## IN A NUTSHELL

Two sets of identical twins, separated as children, are reunited after a lot of mistaken-identity shenanigans.

## OTHER NOTABLE CHARACTERS

Angelo, a goldsmith, becomes part of the confusion when he gives a gold chain to the wrong Antipholus.

## BODY COUNT

None, though Egeon must be feeling a bit worried as the time of his execution gets nearer.

---

### DID YOU KNOW?

❖ *The Comedy of Errors* is Shakespeare's shortest play at just 1,785 lines long. You can fit two-and-a-bit *Errors* into one *Hamlet*.

❖ It was first performed in 1594, but possibly written as early as 1591.

❖ There are several adaptations, including: Rodgers and Hart's musical *The Boys from Syracuse*; the movie *Big Business*, starring Bette Midler and Lily Tomlin; an Indian film called *Double Di Trouble*; and a hip-hop musical, *The Bomb-itty of Errors*.

❖ The plot is adapted from two very old plays, *Menaechmi* and *Amphitruo*, by the Roman playwright Plautus.

❖ This play is one of only two (*The Tempest* is the other) to obey some of the rules of classical theatre by using a single plot which takes place in one day and in one place.

## QUOTABLE LINES

*'Every why hath a wherefore.'*

*'Marry, he must have a long spoon
that must eat with the devil.'*

*'I to the world am like a drop of water
That in the ocean seeks another drop.'*
**(ANTIPHOLUS S., ON WISHING HE COULD
FIND HIS MISSING BROTHER)**

# CYMBELINE

In the First Folio *Cymbeline* was listed amongst the tragedies, but it reads like a classic Shakespearean comedy caper – admittedly with a bittersweet undertone. Modern *Complete Works* which separate the plays by category (such as *The Riverside Shakespeare*) tend to put it in with the comedies, and I've followed that example. *Cymbeline* contains echoes of many other plays, both comic and tragic: separated lovers (*Romeo and Juliet*), a baddie encouraging sexual jealousy (*Othello*), a faithful wife maligned (*Much Ado About Nothing*), nobles living in the woods (*As You Like It*), an ageing king losing the plot over his daughter (*King Lear*), a girl dressed as a boy (*Twelfth Night*, *The Merchant of Venice*, etc.) and mistaken identity (too many to mention).

## PLOT

Cymbeline, King of Britain, wants his daughter Imogen (sometimes spelled Innogen) to marry Cloten, vile son of his vile new wife. But Imogen secretly marries nice-but-poor Posthumus. Cymbeline exiles Posthumus to Italy, where he falls in with a rotter called Giacomo (sometimes spelled Iachimo). Giacomo bets Posthumus that, women being faithless, he'll be able to have his way with Imogen. Who knows why Posthumus agrees to this bet.

Giacomo wangles his way into the British court and aggressively pursues Imogen, but she rebuffs his advances as effectively as she does with the persistent Cloten. Undeterred, Giacomo hides in a chest in her bedroom and steals her bracelet. He also does a quick recce of her sleeping body so he can trick Posthumus into thinking he's done the deed (noting a mole on her left breast, the creep). Posthumus falls for Giacomo's lies, and sends word to his servant, Pisanio, to kill Imogen. But Pisanio warns Imogen, and encourages her to dress as a boy and find her husband. Imogen, giving herself the subtle name of Fidele (faithful), is soon lost in the wild Welsh countryside. In one of those Shakespearean coincidences, she stumbles upon her two long-lost brothers Guiderius and Arviragus (though she doesn't know it's them). They're living in a cave with Belarius, who they think is their father (actually, he kidnapped them when they were little, to avenge his banishment).

Belarius and the brothers run into Cloten, who's looking for Imogen, intending to rape her. A fight breaks out, and Guiderius kills Cloten, solving at least one problem. A new one arises, meanwhile, as Imogen, feeling unwell, drinks a dodgy potion and falls into a deathlike slumber. When she wakes, she mistakes the beheaded body of Cloten for Posthumus's. In despair, she joins an invading Roman Army. Posthumus is one of their number, but he swaps sides and fights bravely for Britain, not caring if he's killed, for he's full of regret at the news of Imogen's 'death'. When the Romans are defeated, Posthumus lets himself be taken prisoner.

But it's happy endings all round! The prisoners are brought to Cymbeline, and everyone's true identity is revealed. Posthumus and Imogen are reunited, Cymbeline recovers his lost sons, and Belarius and Giacomo are forgiven. Just when you thought it couldn't get any better, the evil Queen dies.

## IN A NUTSHELL

Two lovers are separated, but after a series of mishaps and mistaken identity, all is well. (This actually sums up quite a few other plays.)

## OTHER NOTABLE CHARACTERS

Filario, with whom Posthumus stays while exiled in Italy. Jupiter, the god, who sends visions to Posthumus.

## BODY COUNT

Cloten and the Queen. That'll teach 'em to be mean.

## DID YOU KNOW?

❖ *Cymbeline* is one of the last plays, probably written around 1610, shortly before *The Tempest*.

❖ *Cymbeline*'s length, labyrinthine plotting and crazily uneven tone have long been a source of irritation to some ('stagy trash of the lowest melodramatic order,' huffed George Bernard Shaw). Many others, though, regard it as charming and other-worldly. It was a favourite of Keats, while Hazlitt thought it 'delightful' and described it as a 'dramatic romance'.

❖ There was a real British King called Cunobeline (sometimes Cymbeline) towards the end of the first century BC. There is little crossover between his life and the events of the play, however.

❖ Posthumus was given his odd name because his father died before he was born.

❖ *Cymbeline* is the only one of Shakespeare's plays to be set predominantly in Wales. Imogen becomes lost in the Welsh hills (which of us hasn't?) after trying to flee to Milford Haven, or 'blessèd Milford' as she calls it.

## QUOTABLE LINES

*'Fear no more the heat o' th' sun,*
*Nor the furious winter's rages;*
*Thou thy worldly task hast done,*
*Home art gone and ta'en thy wages.*
*Golden lads and girls all must,*
*As chimney-sweepers, come to dust.'*
(LINES FROM THIS FAMOUS FUNERAL SONG,
WHICH GUIDERIUS INTONES OVER THE BODY
OF FIDELE/IMOGEN, HAVE BEEN QUOTED
IN VIRGINIA WOOLF'S *MRS DALLOWAY*
AND SAMUEL BECKETT'S *HAPPY DAYS*.)

*'I have not slept one wink.'*

*'As chaste as unsunned snow.'*

## SHAKESPEARE AND ME

*Ros Barber is a writer and novelist whose award-winning verse novel* The Marlowe Papers *explored the idea of Christopher Marlowe as the author of Shakespeare's plays. She's Director of Research at the Shakespearean Authorship Trust and editor of* 30-Second Shakespeare.

**What was your switch-on moment?**

At school I studied Shakespeare as a necessity (enjoying the most quotable parts of *Julius Caesar*, but not falling in love) and during my BA I chose a Shakespeare option simply because I felt ignorant on our most culturally important writer. I did not fall in love with Shakespeare until I started researching *The Marlowe Papers*, which necessitated getting familiar with the entire canon. You might think it ironic that I didn't fall in love with Shakespeare until I was considering the idea that the works were written by Christopher Marlowe, but this was when the language came alive for me, when themes of dual and mistaken identity, exile and thought-dead-but-not-dead characters began to have real resonance.

**Which is your favourite of Shakespeare's plays?**
Perhaps very unfashionably, *Cymbeline*.

**Tell us about the most memorable performance you've seen.**

I was fortunate enough to see Mark Rylance prancing about in his pyjamas in *Hamlet* on my first visit to the Globe. There are few more memorable than that. But last year I went to the Oregon Shakespeare Festival and saw *Much Ado* with Rex Young as an unforgettable Dogberry, zipping about on a Segway. That one will stay with me too.

> **Which Shakespeare character would you most like to meet?**
> Touchstone. My favourite fool.

# LOVE'S LABOUR'S LOST

*LLL* is a sparkling satire full of witty wordplay, yet insubstantial as candyfloss. It's been described as Shakespeare's 'Seinfeldian' comedy because nothing happens. (Not that there's anything wrong with that.) It has no big plot devices, no shipwrecks or murders, just an uneven battle of the sexes (the women were always going to win), some classic misunderstandings with disguises and letters, and a whole lotta rhyming.

## PLOT

Ferdinand, the King of Navarre, and his three lords vow to spend the next three years in celibate scholarship. To assist with this cockamamie scheme, Ferdinand announces that women will not be allowed within a mile of the court. One of the lords, Biron (sometimes spelled Berowne), reminds him that he's meant to be meeting the Princess of France that day, so the King and lords arrange to see her outside the court. Then pompous visitor Don Armado tells the King that the Fool, Costard, has been caught with Jaquenetta, a country lass. The King instructs Don Armado to punish Costard, and sallies off. Don Armado sneakily offers Costard a reprieve if he'll deliver Jaquenetta a letter from him, for he's in love with her too.

The Princess is pretty irritated at being refused entry to the court. She and her three ladies charm the King and his lords, and the men fall to pieces. Lord Biron likes Rosaline, Lord Longueville fancies Maria and Lord Dumaine is aflutter for Catherine. King Ferdinand is, naturally, rather attracted to the Princess.

Biron asks Costard to deliver a letter to Rosaline, and there's some comedy when that letter gets muddled with the one from Don Armado. There's also much mickey-taking of the King when he's caught composing love poems to the Princess. The randy courtiers give up on their short-lived celibacy vows and disguise themselves to woo the ladies. The women, who are wise to this, disguise themselves too, as each other, and confusion ensues. The men, realising they are beat, promise to be more honest in future. Then they all watch a play, performed by Don Armado and some others, but it's interrupted with news of the Princess's father's death. The women depart, with promises that if the men behave properly, they'll consider their marriage proposals in a year's time.


## IN A NUTSHELL

In deciding to take a vow of celibacy, the King and his lords haven't reckoned with the allure and wily natures of the women.


## OTHER NOTABLE CHARACTERS

Boyet is a French lord in the Princess's party who acts as go-between. And Dull is the policeman, who isn't the sharpest tool in the box.

## BODY COUNT

The Princess of France's father, though it's hard to care too much, as we never see him.

---

### DID YOU KNOW?

❖ *Love's Labour's Lost* contains the longest single scene in any of the plays: the final scene (Act 5, Scene 2) is a staggering 1,016 lines.

❖ Over 60 per cent of the lines are rhymed, more than any other play by some distance. It also contains more words not previously used by Shakespeare than any of the other plays.

❖ First performed for Elizabeth I around 1596, the play was popular with early audiences but lost its way. It's one of the few Shakespeare plays not to have been performed at all in the eighteenth century.

❖ Journalist and critic Bernard Levin apparently once said that the intensity of the ecstasy experienced from an open-air production was on a par only with sexual pleasure. Steady on, Bernard!

---

## QUOTABLE LINES

*'Light, seeking light, doth light of light beguile.'*

*'At Christmas I no more desire a rose*
*Than wish a snow in May's new-fangled shows,*
*But like of each thing that in season grows.'*

*'A high hope for a low heaven.'*

# MEASURE FOR MEASURE

Another of the 'problem' comedies – in fact, the first one so named – *Measure for Measure* has a hefty undertone of cynicism. No one actually dies, but it's a close call. Set in brothels and prisons, with pimps, prostitutes and – much worse – power-crazed hypocrites, and with themes of sex and corruption, this is Shakespeare's walk on the wild side.

## PLOT

The Duke of Vienna, Vincentio, leaves the city in the care of a judge called Angelo – then disguises himself as a friar and stays around to see what sort of a job Angelo makes of it. Angelo's first action is to call for the demolition of the brothels; his second, to pass a law punishing fornication with death (a bit harsh). He immediately sentences to death a fellow called Claudio for having done the naughty with the now-pregnant Juliet. The two were betrothed, to be fair, but not yet legally married. Damn paperwork.

Claudio's friend Lucio asks Isabella, Claudio's sister, to beg Angelo for mercy on her brother's behalf. Isabella is a novice nun, so naturally is shocked when Angelo proposes a bargain: if Isabella sleeps with him, he'll pardon Claudio. She refuses, and visits Claudio in prison to tell him. She's understandably outraged when Claudio asks her if she won't consider taking one for the team, to spare his life. Overhearing this, the Friar (the Duke in disguise) offers to help. He knows that Angelo was going to marry a woman called Mariana, but broke off the engagement when she lost her dowry. Angelo isn't coming out of this well, is he? So the Duke arranges a 'bed trick', in which Isabella lets Angelo know that she's up for it, as long as it's in the dark. But Mariana takes her place. Despite believing that he's bedded Isabella, that louse Angelo breaks his promise, demanding that Claudio be executed and his head be sent to him. The Duke/Friar then performs another bit of magic, known as a 'head trick': he arranges for the head of another prisoner, who has recently died of fever, to be sent in place of Claudio's.

There's some funny business running through this, with Lucio slagging off the Duke to the Friar, and later, being rude about the Friar to the Duke. When the Duke 'returns' to Vienna (i.e. whips off his Friar's habit), he listens to Isabella and Mariana's charges against Angelo, who denies everything. The Duke pops out and returns as the Friar, but when his true identity is revealed, Angelo realises he'll now be exposed as a lying fiend, and begs to be executed. The Duke tells him he has to marry Mariana first, so she gets his fortune. But rather unexpectedly, Mariana begs for Angelo to be pardoned. The Duke reveals that Claudio is still alive and agrees to spare Angelo. He then punishes the bad-mouthing Lucio by making him marry a prostitute who he slept with but refused to marry. The Duke then – in an about-turn that surprises everyone, not least the audience – proposes marriage to Isabella. She remains enigmatically silent.

## IN A NUTSHELL

Men, huh! They're all the same. Oh, and power corrupts.

## OTHER NOTABLE CHARACTERS

Mistress Overdone, a madam, who's upset that the brothels might be closed. The brilliantly named Pompey Bum, a pimp who pretends to be a bartender.

## BODY COUNT

Lots of people *think* they're going to be executed: Claudio, Lucio and, later, Angelo. But the only person who dies during the play is the chap whose head replaces Claudio's, and he apparently died of natural causes. Another prisoner, Barnardine, is approached first to see if he's willing to give up his head for a noble cause but, oddly, he isn't keen.

## DID YOU KNOW?

❖ The title comes from the Bible: 'For with what judgement ye judge, ye shall be judged: and with what measure ye mete, it shall be measured to you again' (Matthew 7:2).

❖ Tennyson's poem 'Mariana' is about the character in *Measure for Measure*, and describes her sadness at Angelo's abandonment.

❖ The ending, in which the Duke asks Isabella to marry him and she says nothing, can be played in many ways. Is she speechless with joy at his proposal, or silent in despair and disbelief that none of the chaps can keep his feelings in his trousers? A canny director and actor can spin out Isabella's silence, leaving it unresolved, or have her shrug or shake her head; on such a small gesture the whole resolution of the play hangs.

 QUOTABLE LINES

*'When he makes water,*
*his urine is congealed ice.'*
**(LUCIO TALKING ABOUT ANGELO.**
**ONE OF SHAKESPEARE'S GREATEST INSULTS.)**

*'What's mine is yours,*
*and what is yours is mine.'*

*'Some rise by sin,*
*and some by virtue fall.'*

*'Condemn the fault,*
*and not the actor of it!'*

# THE MERCHANT OF VENICE

*The Merchant of Venice* can make modern audiences squirm. The play has troubling tones of anti-Semitism, with Shylock, the Jewish moneylender, cruelly humiliated. We might attempt to excuse Shakespeare for being caught up in the prevailing view of Jews at the time, or we might not. However, there is another way of looking at it, which is that Shakespeare, that great humanizer, presents Shylock as a very real and tragic man, the most three-dimensional character in the entire play, giving him one of the great speeches to boot: 'If you prick us, do we not bleed?' A good director can do wonders with this uneasy-making play, helping us make sense of Shylock's complexities. It's another problem play which doesn't really fit into any one category: undoubtedly funny, upsetting and also quite fanciful – improbable, fairy-tale-like things happen in it.

## PLOT

The merchant of the title is Antonio, who owns a fleet of sailing ships. He's a sad fellow, though we never get to the bottom of his melancholy (some have speculated that it's because he's secretly in love with his dear – but straight – friend Bassanio). Though wealthy on paper, he's cash-poor, so when Bassanio asks for money to woo Portia, a wealthy heiress, Antonio arranges to borrow it from Shylock, the moneylender. Portia's late father left one of those tricksy wills which says she can only marry the man who chooses correctly from three clue-laden caskets.

Antonio's unlikely deal with Shylock states that if he cannot pay back the borrowed 3,000 ducats, Shylock can take a pound of Antonio's flesh. The two men have some history: Antonio has publicly accused Shylock of charging excessive interest. Shylock admits in an aside that he also hates Antonio because he's a Christian (this line is sometimes cut as it's hard to build a sympathetic portrait of Shylock with it in).

Meanwhile, suitors come and go at Portia's, selecting the wrong caskets and losing the chance to marry her. Portia tells Bassanio to take his time choosing, which she sure as eggs hasn't told the others. He chooses the correct – lead – casket, and they delightedly marry.

Inevitably, Antonio's ships are lost at sea and he cannot meet his debt. Shylock already has a black temper on him, because his beloved daughter Jessica has run off with Antonio's friend Lorenzo, taking a large amount of Shylock's fortune with her. So he insists on getting his pound of flesh, even when Bassanio shows up with enough money to pay Antonio's debt twice over. Just when Shylock is wielding a knife dangerously close to Antonio's heart, Portia (disguised as a lawyer called Balthasar) steps forward to point out that no blood was in the deal; if Shylock spills one drop, the deal is void. It's like a sixteenth-century *The Good Wife*, in which a legal technicality wrecks an entire case. Shylock backtracks, saying he will, after all, accept Bassanio's alternative offer. But it's too late. The Duke presiding over the trial rules that Shylock must hand over half his wealth and convert to Christianity. The play ends with merry japes when Portia reveals to Bassanio that she was Balthasar all along.

## IN A NUTSHELL

Stereotyped Jew insists on his pound of flesh and is humiliated.

## OTHER NOTABLE CHARACTERS

Nerissa, Portia's lady-in-waiting, a spirited gal like her mistress, dresses up as Balthasar's clerk.

## BODY COUNT

None, though Antonio must think his number is up when the alarmed Bassanio says to Shylock, 'Why dost thou whet thy knife so earnestly?'

---

### DID YOU KNOW?

❖ Although there were almost no Jews in Shakespeare's England, having been expelled in 1290 by Edward I, they were still popular figures of hate. *Merchant of Venice* was first performed around 1597, just three years after Queen Elizabeth's Portuguese-Jewish doctor, Roderigo Lopez, was convicted of plotting her murder.

❖ The pound-of-flesh tale is an ancient one, while Shakespeare was probably influenced by Christopher Marlowe's *The Jew of Malta* and an Italian collection of stories called *Il Pecorone*.

❖ Hamlet apart, no character has inspired more critical commentary than Shylock. He's one of Shakespeare's great, complex roles, both aggressor and victim.

❖ Shylock's dead wife, Leah, is barely mentioned, but when she is, it's richly poignant. Shylock hears that daughter Jessica has sold a turquoise ring she stole from him to buy a monkey. 'I had it of Leah when I was a bachelor,' he says of the ring. 'I would not have given it for a wilderness of monkeys.' In discussing his book *Shylock*

---

*Is My Name*, Howard Jacobson says we're allowed a glimpse of Shylock here as the man he was before he became the man we see now.

❖ It's not clear precisely how much 3,000 ducats would have been worth in Shakespeare's day, but it would have been a lot – equivalent to an annual income.

## QUOTABLE LINES

*'Hath not a Jew eyes? Hath not a Jew hands, organs, dimensions, senses, affections, passions…?'*

**SHYLOCK'S FAMOUS SPEECH**
**CONTINUES A LITTLE LATER:**
*'If you prick us do we not bleed? If you tickle us do we not laugh? If you poison us do we not die? And if you wrong us shall we not revenge?'*

*'The devil can cite Scripture for his purpose.'*

*'The quality of mercy is not strained.'*

*'But love is blind.'*

*'All that glisters is not gold.'*
**(THIS IS THE CLUE ON THE GOLDEN CASKET,**
**OFTEN MISQUOTED AS 'ALL THAT GLITTERS'.)**

# THE MERRY WIVES OF WINDSOR

*The Merry Wives of Windsor* sees the welcome return of Falstaff, the great carouser from *Henry IV* (*Parts I* and *II*). He was reported dead in *Henry V* but is brought to life here, a couple of centuries later, for one more glass of sack wine. Falstaff is one of Shakespeare's most enduring, and endearing, characters: large, witty, drunken and devil-may-care. He steals all the *Henry IV* scenes he's in, so no doubt audiences would have been delighted to see him in a leading role. *Merry Wives* is one of the most light-hearted of the comedies, but it divides the critics, with some describing it as Shakespeare's weakest play, and others praising its humour and deft plotting.

## PLOT

Sir John Falstaff has a cash-flow problem. So he decides to woo two rich married ladies (the 'merry wives'), Alice Ford and Margaret Page, who he is sure will shower him with gifts from their husbands' coffers. He writes them letters, identical other than the names at the top. But the two women swap notes, literally, and are annoyed that he assumes they'll both be so easily sweet-talked into betraying their hubbies with a fat old fellow. However, they agree it'll be funny to pretend to go along with it.

Pistol and Nym, two disgruntled members of Falstaff's entourage, reveal his adulterous plan to the husbands. Master Page is cool about it, but Master Ford is a jealous type. He pretends to be a chap called Mr Brooke, telling Falstaff that he too loves Mistress Ford and that if Falstaff gets her into bed he, 'Brooke', will be more likely to able to tempt her too. A delighted Falstaff says that he's already on it.

The women trick Falstaff into hiding from Master Ford in a basket of smelly laundry, which is then chucked into the Thames. But Falstaff, still convinced the women like him, goes back for more. This time they trick him into disguising himself as an old witch, Mother Prat, who gets beaten by Ford. Finally, the wives confide in their husbands and together they plan a trick in which Falstaff, wearing a silly outfit, will be humiliated by townsfolk in Windsor Park.

Meanwhile, the Pages' young daughter, Anne, has three suitors: Slender, favoured by her father; Caius, who her mother prefers; and Fenton, who Anne herself likes. Master Page tells Slender he can run away with Anne the night they meet to attack Falstaff in the forest, and tells him she'll be dressed as a fairy in white. However, Mistress Page says the same to Caius, except that Anne will be in green.

Poor old Falstaff has a rough time of it in the park, but when the merry wives confess their trickery, he takes it well. Slender and Caius, in the meantime, run off with white and green fairies who turn out to be boys (Caius, the daftie, marries his without realising – at least, that's *his* story), then Anne shows up with Fenton and reveals that they sneaked off and married when no one was looking. Everyone laughs because this is a ker-razy comedy, and they all – including Falstaff – go back to the Pages' house for a drink.

## IN A NUTSHELL

Two wives get the better of Falstaff and their husbands.

## OTHER NOTABLE CHARACTERS

Mistress Quickly, Caius's housekeeper, is given a lot of plot information by young Anne.

## DID YOU KNOW?

❖ *Merry Wives* was apparently written after a request from Queen Elizabeth that she wanted to see Falstaff in love, though this is probably apocryphal.

❖ This is the only one of the comedies set entirely in England.

❖ Catherine the Great wrote a Russian version of *Merry Wives* called *The Basket*, performed in St Petersburg in the 1780s.

❖ Astonishingly, despite everything we know about theatre in Shakespeare's day, Falstaff as Mother Prat is one of only two instances in the plays that a stage direction requests a man to be disguised as a woman (the other is in the opening section to *The Taming of the Shrew*). Usually, the disguises go in the other direction, with women dressing as men.

 QUOTABLE LINES

'Out of my door, you witch, you rag, you baggage, you polecat, you runnion!'
(MASTER FORD TO POOR OLD FALSTAFF, WHEN HE'S DRESSED AS MOTHER PRAT.)

'Why then, the world's mine oyster.'

'There's the long and the short.'

'I cannot tell what the dickens his name is.'

# A MIDSUMMER NIGHT'S DREAM

The most performed of Shakespeare's plays, *A Midsummer Night's Dream* is an intoxicating mix of lovers, fairies, mischief and transformation. It's a romcom with a supernatural edge; a crazy mash-up of different worlds colliding in one dreamy night in the forest.

## PLOT

Theseus, Duke of Athens, is preparing for his wedding day with Hippolyta. But love isn't so simple for others... Lysander loves Hermia, and Hermia loves Lysander. Helena loves Demetrius, but, uh-oh, Demetrius loves... Hermia. Unfortunately, Hermia's father wants her to marry Demetrius. So Hermia and Lysander plan to meet in the forest that night and run away together. Hermia confides in Helena, her best friend, but lovesick Helena tells Demetrius, hoping he'll like her for it. He doesn't, and just hotfoots it after Hermia, with Helena close behind.

The four would-be lovers don't have the woods to themselves. For one, there's a troupe of tradesmen, rehearsing a play they hope to perform at Theseus's wedding; and there's a group of fairies. The Fairy King and Queen, Oberon and Titania, have fallen out. Oberon instructs Puck, his loyal but mischievous servant, to pour the juice of a magical flower into Titania's eyes while she sleeps. This flower makes the sleeper fall in love with the first person they see. Noticing Helena and Demetrius in the forest, Oberon tells Puck to put the juice into Demetrius's eyes also. But Puck mistakenly gives Lysander the juice treatment instead, so that Lysander claps eyes on Helena and falls in love with her. Puck then puts the juice into Demetrius's eyes, so now there are two men chasing a bewildered Helena, while Hermia, who lately had two suitors, now has none. Puck manages to sort things out before there's a fight, and gives Lysander an antidote so he falls back in love with Hermia.

Puck also messes around with the actors (known as 'mechanicals', meaning manual workers or craftsmen). He gives a weaver called Bottom the head of an ass, and Titania, under the flower-juice influence, falls in love with him. Her fairies treat him like a king, and the puzzled Bottom gamely goes along with it. Oberon finally releases Titania from the spell, and Puck sets Bottom back to normal.

The mechanicals get to perform *Pyramus and Thisbe*, their rather poor am-dram, at the wedding, and Theseus declares that Hermia can marry who she likes. *Midsummer* ends with Puck asking the audience to think of the play as if it was all a dream.

## IN A NUTSHELL

All the wrong people love each other, but the fairies sort it out and everyone's happy at the end. Except Hermia's dad. And the wedding guests who have to sit through *Pyramus and Thisbe*.

## OTHER NOTABLE CHARACTERS

The mechanicals are all very funny: Peter Quince, Francis Flute, Tom Snout, Robin Starveling and Snug.

## DID YOU KNOW?

❖ *A Midsummer Night's Dream* has been subjected to more interpretations than any of the plays except perhaps *Hamlet*, with allegorical, feminist, class-based and symbolic readings amongst the many analyses.

❖ There's usually a performance of it on somewhere. The *World Shakespeare Bibliography* calculates that between 1959 and 2015 there were more than 2,000 productions of *A Midsummer Night's Dream*. This doesn't include the innumerable school and am-dram productions, for which the play is much loved because it contains so many small parts.

❖ The grande dame of Titanias is Judi Dench, who first played the part at school in the 1940s; again in the 1960s for Peter Hall's stage and film versions; again in 2010; and then in 2016, at the age of 81, she performed it in a sketch as part of the RSC's 400th anniversary celebrations, playing opposite Al Murray as Bottom.

❖ The Beatles performed *Pyramus and Thisbe* in a TV special in 1964. You can catch this on YouTube, though it's hard to hear over the screaming girls.

❖ The play is based on more sources than any other Shakespeare play, including works by Ovid and Chaucer, amongst several others.

❖ Samuel Pepys wasn't a fan, describing the play in his 1662 diary as 'the most insipid ridiculous play that ever I saw in my life.'

 QUOTABLE LINES

'Lord, what fools these mortals be!'

'The course of true love never did run smooth.'

'Ill met by moonlight, proud Titania.'

'I'll put a girdle round about the earth
In forty minutes.'

'I know a bank where the wild thyme blows.'

'And though she be but little, she is fierce.'
(HELENA TALKING ABOUT HERMIA.
BEING SMALL MYSELF, I HAVE THIS LINE
ON MY FAVOURITE RSC MUG.)

'If we shadows have offended,
Think but this, and all is mended:
That you have but slumbered here,
While these visions did appear.'
(PUCK'S FINAL EXCUSE IF YOU
DIDN'T LIKE THE PLAY.)

# SHAKESPEARE AND ME

*Natasha Hancock is an actress who has played many Shakespearean roles, including Audrey in* As You Like It *at the Globe.*

## What was your switch-on moment?

I can honestly say that I can't remember Shakespeare's works not being part of my consciousness. I was very fortunate to be raised in a family that appreciated his work, and when I went to secondary school my drama teacher was so enthusiastic and encouraging about Shakespeare's work that I never felt hesitant about asking questions.

## Which is your favourite play?

*King Lear.*

## Tell us about the most memorable production you've seen?

It has to be an open-air production of *A Midsummer Night's Dream* I saw in the West Dean grounds. The company were very imaginative, using the woodland walk from the car park to create the atmosphere from the outset by using recordings of laughter, whispers in the branches, and the occasional actor (fairy) running and hiding just out of eyeline to make you wonder whether you'd seen anything. This created a wonderful and magical prologue to the production, which carried on being highly enjoyable and creative.

**Which Shakespeare character have you most enjoyed playing?**

It's a toss-up between Cordelia in *King Lear* and Katherine in *The Taming of the Shrew*.

**How would you persuade somebody to give Shakespeare a chance?**

A lot of people put emphasis on the way Shakespeare wrote, use of iambic pentameter, etc. I'm not saying it isn't important or useful, but it isn't everything. If you read Shakespeare in the same way you would read any other script or story, using his punctuation, you are part way there. If you then look at which words have been used, where and when, talking to which other character, etc., you will unveil the character.

# *MUCH ADO ABOUT NOTHING*

The sparkling banter and relative brevity of *Much Ado* made it very popular in its day, and it continues to be a great favourite. Beatrice and Benedick give actors the chance to fly delicious sparks off each other.

## PLOT

When his friends return from war, kindly nobleman Leonato welcomes them to his house in Messina, Sicily, for a bit of R & R. His daughter Hero and niece Beatrice are excited at the prospect of some handsome male company.

The soldiers are Don Pedro (a prince), Claudio (a nobleman), Benedick (a cheeky chap) and Don John (Don Pedro's illegitimate and sulky brother). Claudio and Hero immediately fall in love and decide to marry in a week – these young 'uns don't hang about. Beatrice and Benedick, meanwhile, are sparring partners of old, and are soon sexily insulting each other and insisting they will never marry. They're tricked by Claudio and Hero into thinking that the other loves them, whereupon they admit to themselves that their name-calling has been hiding true feelings of love.

All would be well if it wasn't for that pesky Don John (boo!). He convinces Claudio that Hero is unfaithful, showing him a woman at a window who he claims is Hero having intimate relations with another man. In fact, the woman is Margaret, Hero's servant, with Don John's henchman, Borachio. But the gullible ass Claudio believes Don John, and on the day of his wedding he angrily accuses Hero of all sorts, publicly humiliating her. Hero swoons, and her family hide her away and let it be known that she has died of grief. Beatrice and Benedick confess their love to each other, and when Benedick says he believes Hero, Beatrice tells him she can't marry him unless he kills Claudio for shaming Hero.

The nightwatchmen overhear Borachio boasting about his involvement in the scandal and he's arrested by the police chief, Dogberry. Benedick challenges Claudio to a duel, but before it takes place, Claudio discovers that Hero was innocent, and is devastated. Don John does a runner, the swine. Leonato tells Claudio that to show his repentance he must marry his niece (not Beatrice), sight unseen. The grieving Claudio agrees, and is amazed and delighted when the veil is lifted to reveal Hero, alive and well. Benedick proposes to Beatrice, they bicker feistily for a while, and then there's a double wedding, made even happier by the news of Don John's arrest.

## IN A NUTSHELL

It's the Beatrice and Benedick Banter Show, plus a cautionary tale about not believing everything baddies tell you about your girlfriend.

## OTHER NOTABLE CHARACTERS

Friar Francis, who supports Hero at the wedding and suggests her family pretend she's died.

---

### DID YOU KNOW?

❖ *Much Ado* is one of the few Shakespeare plays where the majority of the text is written in prose.

❖ Though the wrong done to Hero is technically the main plot, most people have noted that Beatrice and Benedick are considerably more fun, including Charles II, who apparently wrote, *Benedick and Beatrice* beside the play's title in his copy of the Second Folio. Berlioz's celebrated 1862 opera, *Béatrice et Bénédict*, was based on our two favourite sparring lovers.

---

- ❖ Kenneth Branagh's 1993 *Much Ado* film is one of the most successful Shakespeare movies. The opening, in the glorious Italian countryside, with Emma Thompson reading the song 'Sigh No More', is just lovely.

- ❖ It's been speculated that *Much Ado* was known in Shakespeare's day as *Love's Labour's Won* (though this title has also been proposed for other plays).

 QUOTABLE LINES

*'Sigh no more, ladies, sigh no more.*
*Men were deceivers ever.'*

**THIS FAMOUS SONG CONCLUDES:**
*'Then sigh not so, but let them go,*
*And be you blithe and bonny,*
*Converting all your sounds of woe*
*Into hey nonny, nonny.'*

*'He that hath a beard is more than a youth, and*
*he that hath no beard is less than a man.'*

*'When I said I would die a bachelor, I did not*
*think I should live till I were married.'*
**(BENEDICK, OF COURSE.)**

*'Are you good men and true?'*

*'There was never yet philosopher*
*That could endure the toothache patiently.'*

*'Thou and I are too wise to woo peaceably.'*

## SHAKESPEARE AND ME

*Samira Ahmed is a journalist and presenter of*
*Front Row on BBC Radio 4. She broadcast*
*the introduction for a National Theatre Live*
*production of* As You Like It.

### What was your switch-on moment?

We did *Hamlet* for A level and I fell in love. With
the play. With him. It's the perfect play for teens,
isn't it? We were taken to see John Duttine in it, in
Leatherhead around 1984. I was enthralled. Even
now whenever I see it I am blown away by the
way the plot speeds up, and you end with this total
carnage – bodies everywhere. It's amazing.

### Which is your favourite of Shakespeare's plays?

*Much Ado About Nothing.* I love the cracking
romantic exchanges. It's like a Hollywood golden-
age romantic comedy 350 years early. And I love

the darkness in it. Beatrice really wants Benedick to kill Claudio. Through my twenties I would have said *Hamlet*, but I'm so much more unforgiving of his treatment of Ophelia now.

**Tell us about the most memorable performance you've seen.**

Seeing Jonathan Pryce as Shylock at the Globe was like watching the play in two different eras at the same time: the happily anti-Semitic Elizabethan comedy, and a modern vision of Shylock as victim of Establishment bully boys. My eyes are tearing up even thinking of it! And an intense National Youth Theatre production of *Othello* which played Iago as a young racist thug. International productions can pull out the great stories. I saw a terrific kabuki *Twelfth Night*, and a Korean *Midsummer Night's Dream*. But to choose one: Robert Stephens in 1991 as Falstaff in *Henry IV*. He'd lived a kind of Falstaffian existence, which added real poignancy to the performance. He seemed to make eye contact with each of us in the audience. His eyes twinkled as if directly at me.

**Which Shakespeare character would you most like to meet?**

I'd marry Benedick any day. And I'd like to meet the women who hold their own. Lady Percy or Queen Margaret. Or Cordelia, or Queen Gertrude. The most fascinating is the unnamed 'First Servant' in *King Lear* who turns against his masters, and is killed. You're thinking – who is this man?

# PERICLES, PRINCE OF TYRE

If the number of quartos printed in Shakespeare's time is any guide, *Pericles* was a big hit in the early seventeenth century. It didn't make it into the First Folio, though, and has been struggling for exposure and authenticity ever since. It's believed to be a late collaboration with George Wilkins, innkeeper and part-time dramatist, who would otherwise be entirely forgotten. Despite its Cinderella status, the play has its fans. Andrew Dickson describes the ending as 'among Shakespeare's most intensely moving'.

## PLOT

Like *The Taming of the Shrew*, *Pericles* is a story told to the audience by another character. In this case the narrator is the medieval poet John Gower, risen from the grave, who takes us back to the classical-era Middle East. The King of Antioch (unimaginatively called Antiochus) is having incestuous relations with his daughter. He's also seeing off all suitors for her by way of a riddle. Pericles, a prince, works it out; unfortunately the answer reveals the incest. With his ardour for the Princess on the wane, he hints to Antiochus that he knows the truth and skips town. This is wise as he's now pursued by an assassin.

Most of the play involves Pericles travelling, first home to Tyre, then on to Tarsus, the assassin on his heels. Pericles rescues the population of Tarsus from famine, but soon he's off again. He's shipwrecked by a storm and washes up at Pentapolis. Here, despite some rust on his armour, he wins a jousting tournament and the hand of Thaisa, the King's daughter. Things are looking up, as Antiochus has died, meaning assassination is no longer a threat and Pericles can return home.

There is *another* storm on the voyage to Tyre, however, and new bride Thaisa apparently dies in childbirth. Her body is thrown overboard and the grief-stricken Pericles gives his daughter Marina over to the care of friends. Thaisa, though, isn't dead at all. After she's washed ashore, she assumes Pericles has died, and heads off to be a vestal virgin at the temple of Diana.

In the final sequence of the play, Pericles rules in Tyre, while Marina, now grown up, has been kidnapped and sold to a brothel. Pericles encounters Marina during her escape and eventually realises who she is. All that's left is to contrive a meeting between Pericles and Thaisa and, following their mutual recognition, for the rejoicing to start.

## IN A NUTSHELL

Pericles wins a princess, flees for his life, then wins another. Following a shipwreck and some misunderstandings, he's reunited with his wife and daughter.

## OTHER NOTABLE CHARACTERS

Wise old Helicanus, Pericles's adviser, who acts as regent in Tyre, keeps him up to date on murder plots and the like, and is unwaveringly loyal.

## BODY COUNT

Presumably there's some collateral damage from the shipwrecks. Otherwise it's mainly characters wrongly thinking other characters are dead.

---

### DID YOU KNOW?

❖ Though plenty has been written about the symbolism of weather in the plays, storm-induced accidents seem simply to be a way of geeing a story along. As well as the two shipwrecks in *Pericles* (one too many, perhaps), *The Tempest* is set in motion by Prospero's storm, and both *Twelfth Night* and *The Comedy of Errors* rely on characters being separated following a mishap at sea.

❖ Shakespeare apparently collaborated with other writers more frequently from the mid-1600s onwards. Shakespearean scholar James Shapiro reckons he had time to do this because the King's Men felt he was better employed writing than acting. Or at least that's what they said to his face. (Tributes to his thespian talents aren't a big part of the historical record.)

## QUOTABLE LINES

### THE RIDDLE PERICLES
### SOLVES IS AS FOLLOWS:

*'I am no viper, yet I feed
On mother's flesh which did me breed.
I sought a husband, in which labour
I found that kindness in a father.
He's father, son, and husband mild;
I mother, wife, and yet his child.
How they may be and yet in two,
As you will live resolve it you.'*

# THE TAMING OF THE SHREW

It's easy to forget – I certainly did (and perhaps Shakespeare did too) – that this is a play within a play. All the action with Kate being 'tamed' by Petruccio is actually a show presented to a befuddled tinker. Being at one remove isn't quite enough to excuse it, though. It's one of the most difficult plays for a modern audience, who can feel rather awkward watching a spirited woman being subjugated and abused. As always with Shakespeare, a smart director can make it work however they want, and there are numerous feminist interpretations and versions. But it's still hard to know what to do with Kate's last speech, in which she agrees that a woman's place is under a man's thumb.

## PLOT

The play opens with Christopher Sly, a poor tinker, who is out-of-his-tree drunk. A lord who encounters him decides to play a trick on him – this is an additional uncomfortable aspect of the play, generally lost in all the other uncomfortable aspects. The lord's servants tell Sly that *he* is a lord, set him up in comfy chambers belonging to the real lord and wait on him until he believes them. Then some travelling players come in, and Sly settles down to watch. The players perform *The Taming of the Shrew*, the plot of which is as follows.

Bianca is a mild-mannered young woman with several suitors, but father Baptista says she can't marry until her older sister Katherine does. Katherine is a sharp-tongued lass, which has put off the wimpy males of Padua. However, newly arrived Petruccio is undeterred by her reputation – and, more to the point, intrigued by her substantial dowry. When the two meet, they have a verbal scrap, and sparks fly. Petruccio tells Baptista that Katherine has agreed to marry him. She hasn't, but is uncharacteristically silent on the matter. Petruccio is late to their wedding and behaves oddly from the off, wearing strange clothes and whisking her away before the feast. He puts her in a house far from her family and continues to 'tame' her by preventing her from eating or sleeping. In classic domestic-abuser style, he tells her this is because the food and bed aren't good enough for someone he loves as much as her.

Meanwhile, Lucentio, also newly arrived in Padua, has fallen for Bianca. He disguises himself as a Latin schoolmaster for her. This idea also occurs to another of Bianca's suitors, Hortensio, who disguises himself as a music teacher. (How young actually is Bianca?) She finally chooses Lucentio, and they marry. Katherine and Petruccio return to Padua, and everyone is shocked to see how thoroughly subservient Kate is. At a banquet to celebrate

Hortensio's marriage to a wealthy widow, Petruccio wins a bet that he has the most obedient wife, and everyone agrees it's a tremendous victory. Kate delivers a speech in which she says how important it is for a woman to obey her husband.

We never return to Christopher Sly, but end instead with Lucentio wondering if Bianca is quite as obedient a wife as he had hoped.

## IN A NUTSHELL

A strong-willed woman is beaten down by marriage.

## OTHER NOTABLE CHARACTERS

Tranio, Lucentio's servant, who's disguised as his master for a large part of the play so that Lucentio can play the part of Bianca's teacher.

## BODY COUNT

None, unless you count the murdered spirit of poor old Kate.

### DID YOU KNOW?

❖ Some chronologies list *The Taming of the Shrew* as Shakespeare's second play, in 1590, after *The Two Gentlemen of Verona*.

❖ The fact that the play as it appears in the First Folio doesn't return at the end to its framing device with Christopher Sly might have been the oversight of a novice playwright. In 1594 a play with the same name had a final scene with Sly.

❖ The first ever Shakespeare talkie was *The Taming of the Shrew*, with Mary Pickford and Douglas Fairbanks.

❖ There are many ways to interpret Kate's 'taming', including the notion that Shakespeare was attempting to satirise how cruel society could be to women; that the difficult Katherine learned to be a better person; that she was pretending to be tamed; that both parties found the verbal back and forth erotic; that she had been driven quite mad; or that she was a battered wife. Your choice.

## QUOTABLE LINES

*'There's small choice in rotten apples.'*

*'Thereby hangs a tale.'*

*'We will have rings, and things, and fine array;*
*And kiss me, Kate. We will be married o' Sunday.'*

*'If I be waspish, best beware my sting.'*

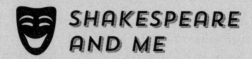

# SHAKESPEARE AND ME

*Nicola Hawley is an education officer at the Shakespeare Birthplace Trust, with responsibility for the programme for primary schoolchildren.*

### What was your switch-on moment?

When I was 13, my parents took me to an RSC performance of *As You Like It*. It was an inspired choice, a play that had everything: banishment, mistaken identities and countless amusing misunderstandings. I was immediately entranced by the outstanding performance, the beautiful scenery and Shakespeare's words and wit. I was hooked from that moment on!

### Which is your favourite of Shakespeare's plays?

*Antony and Cleopatra*. I studied it at school and found this love story compelling. In a play filled with power struggles, war and political intrigue, I have always been fascinated by the relationship between Antony and Cleopatra and their ultimate destruction.

### Tell us about the most memorable performance you've seen.

It was a performance of *The Taming of the Shrew* in 2003. It was a play I had always disliked, mainly because of the humiliations heaped on Katherine. However, the character played by Alexandra Gilbreath on that evening was never the victim of Petruccio's misogyny. The audience was left in no doubt that she was, in every respect, more than his equal, and at the end of the play the audience rose as one to applaud her. It was a truly memorable performance.

## Which Shakespeare character would you most like to meet?

I would love to meet Henry V, and hear his account of the Battle of Agincourt and how much poetic licence was used in the play. In my role at the Shakespeare Birthplace Trust, I endeavour to bring history to life. Children love stories about heroes, kings and battles, and *Henry V* gives us all of these.

## How would you persuade somebody to give Shakespeare a chance?

It is important to look at the plays in the context of the time in which they were written. If you are able to visit Stratford-upon-Avon and walk in Shakespeare's footsteps – by visiting his childhood home, seeing the schoolroom where he received his education, the church where he was baptised, worshipped and is buried – and see a performance of his work at the theatre, then you will discover more about the ordinary man who went on to do extraordinary things. Many of the messages in Shakespeare's works still resonate today; his histories are interesting, his tragedies are compelling and his comedies are still very funny.

# THE TEMPEST

Widely believed to be the final play Shakespeare wrote solo, *The Tempest* is certainly his last major work. It contains some beautiful poetry, and is full of gentle, weary uncertainties. It's tempting to think of it as his swansong, partly because the speech beginning 'Our revels now are ended' is an unbeatable farewell.

## PLOT

A storm is conjured up by Prospero, magician and erstwhile Duke of Milan, now banished to an unspecified, possibly Mediterranean, island with his daughter Miranda. The aim of the tempest is to shipwreck the usurper of the dukedom, Prospero's brother Alonso, and his co-conspirator, Antonio, the King of Naples.

Prospero's spirit servant, Ariel, has ensured the castaways are safe but scattered across the island. Prospero is also served by the monster Caliban, initially an ally but now in forced servitude following the attempted rape of Miranda. Neither Ariel nor Caliban is exactly thrilled at their state. Caliban finds two sailors to assist him in a coup against Prospero, seeing their alcohol as powerful magic. He fails to notice that their plan is to kidnap and exhibit him (the man-beast) for a quick buck back home.

Prospero, assisted by Ariel, arranges for Miranda to meet and fall in love with Ferdinand, Antonio's son; though first he enslaves the young man, as many prospective fathers-in-law would love to do. There are also some political shenanigans between Antonio and Alonso. In between magical balls and illusory feasts, Prospero, aided by fancy transformations from Ariel, manages all threats, forgives those who have schemed against him and decides Ferdinand is worthy of his daughter. He releases Ariel, says he's done with magic and invites the applause of the audience to set him free to return to Milan.

## IN A NUTSHELL

Deposed duke uses magical powers to bring his enemies to his island of exile, thwarts plots against him, sets up the marriage of his daughter and heads back to his dukedom.

## OTHER NOTABLE CHARACTERS

Stefano and Trinculo, drunken sailors from central casting and a very bad influence on Caliban. And Gonzalo, a relentlessly cheerful adviser to Alonso.

## BODY COUNT

Despite the storm and various assassination plots, no one actually dies.

---

### DID YOU KNOW?

❖ It seems likely that *The Tempest* was written for the indoor Blackfriars Theatre, around 1610 or 1611. This would have been a better venue than the Globe for the music and special effects.

---

❖ *The Tempest* contains the most music of any Shakespeare play, and has inspired a great deal more, including numerous recordings of the songs 'Where the Bee Sucks' and 'Full Fathom Five'. Composers including Sibelius, Tchaikovsky and Berlioz have based music on *The Tempest*. Percy Bysshe Shelley, Robert Browning and W. H. Auden all wrote *Tempest*-inspired poems.

❖ For many years, Caliban, rather than Prospero, was considered the starring role. Nineteenth-century actor-impresario Frank Benson apparently played Caliban with monkey-like movements and a real fish in his mouth.

❖ *The Tempest* has inspired many film adaptations. One of the most successful was the 1956 sci-fi film *Forbidden Planet*; and one of the most daring, Peter Greenaway's *Prospero's Books* (1991), in which narrator John Gielgud, a famous Prospero, spoke over an extravaganza of peeing infants and writhing naked bodies.

❖ More recently, Prospero has been played by actresses such as Vanessa Redgrave (the Globe in 2000) and Helen Mirren ('Prospera' in a 2010 film version).

❖ It's reckoned that Shakespeare was inspired by an account of a shipwreck by an admiral called Sir George Somers, which took place off the coast of Bermuda.

## QUOTABLE LINES

'Misery acquaints a man with
strange bedfellows.'

'Full fathom five thy father lies.
Of his bones are coral made.'

'How beauteous mankind is! O brave new world
That has such people in 't!'

'Our revels now are ended. These our actors,
As I foretold you, were all spirits, and
Are melted into air, into thin air;

And like the baseless fabric of this vision,
The cloud-capped towers, the gorgeous palaces,
The solemn temples, the great globe itself,
Yea, all which it inherit, shall dissolve;

And, like this insubstantial pageant faded,
Leave not a rack behind. We are such stuff
As dreams are made on, and our little life
Is rounded with a sleep.'

## SHAKESPEARE AND ME

*Ben Crystal is an actor and the author of various books about Shakespeare, including* Shakespeare on Toast *and the* Oxford Illustrated Shakespeare Dictionary, *co-authored with David Crystal. He's also the artistic director of the Passion in Practice theatre ensemble.*

### What was your switch-on moment?

I'd really disliked Shakespeare in school. My catching-a-wave moment was when I was 17, waiting to come on as Ariel in *The Tempest* at an amphitheatre in North Wales. I was wearing a flimsy costume, covered in gold paint, and it was raining. I jumped on stage and it all just made sense. My life changed irrevocably.

### Which is your favourite of Shakespeare's plays?

Ironically, given I struggled so much with it at school, it's *King Lear*. I have a quote from it tattooed on my arm: 'Nothing will come of nothing.' It reminds me that I have to get out of bed and make things happen. *Lear* has a great plot, and is one of the most beautiful and dark of the plays, the tragedy delicately balanced by good lumps of comedy. The language varies from prose to poetry to song, and every character feels fully fleshed out.

**Tell us about the most memorable performance you've seen.**

*Pericles* in Japanese, directed by Yukio Ninagawa, and a joyful Slovakian production of *The Merry Wives of Windsor*. The plays seem very releasing in a foreign language. Then there was Ian Holm in *Lear* – I queued for 12 hours to get a ticket. It was absolutely transformative. And finally, Mark Rylance doing 'To be or not to be' at the Globe.

**Which Shakespeare character have you most enjoyed playing?**

I loved playing Pericles recently. And I was surprised by how much I enjoyed playing Hamlet. It's a truly huge, intense part that should come with a warning: 'This play may seriously affect you and the lives of those around you.'

**How would you persuade somebody to give Shakespeare a chance?**

Read *Shakespeare on Toast*! It's a short, accessible book, which reminds people that in Shakespeare's time, 80 per cent of people couldn't read. The plays were meant to be seen, not read. We wouldn't expect anyone other than a great musician to read a score of music and understand what the tune might sound like. So why do we expect younglings to get Shakespeare by looking at the words? They're being given the score rather than the CD. They need to speak it and hear it.

# TWELFTH NIGHT

Like *The Comedy of Errors* and *The Tempest*, *Twelfth Night* is a tale of separation and rediscovery, set in motion by a storm at sea. No one knows for sure why Shakespeare was so fond of this device, but the theatre company probably had some nautical props lying around and, you know, waste not...

## PLOT

Count Orsino is a lovesick nobleman from Illyria, approximately modern Croatia. Orsino pines for the beautiful Olivia, who is mourning her brother and definitely not entertaining suitors.

We next encounter a young noblewoman, Viola, shipwrecked off the coast. Assuming that her twin brother, Sebastian, has been killed in the wreck, she goes off to seek employment. As Olivia isn't hiring, Viola pretends to be a man, Cesario, and works for Orsino instead. Swiftly it's established that Cesario (Viola) fancies Orsino and, when Orsino sends him/her to Olivia as an emissary, that Olivia similarly has the hots for Cesario. All three are therefore miserable with unrequited love.

We then plunge into a subplot centring around the more high-spirited members of Olivia's household, led by her boozy uncle Sir Toby Belch and the self-regarding Sir Andrew Aguecheek. They play a practical joke on the pompous Malvolio, Olivia's steward, convincing him that Olivia loves him and has a weakness for a man sporting yellow stockings and crossed garters. Suffice to say, this doesn't go well, with Olivia thinking Malvolio is mad, while the others lock him up and mock him.

Viola's brother Sebastian then shows up alive, well and ready to be mistaken for his drag-clad sister. Sir Andrew, who's keen on Olivia (who isn't?), jealously challenges Cesario to a duel.

He ends up fighting Sebastian in error and is only stopped by Olivia entering. She proposes to Sebastian on the spot (mistaken identity again) and, because she's clearly a babe, he agrees immediately. There's also some mixed-up stuff the other way with Viola/Cesario letting Sebastian's friend Antonio get arrested by Orsino and, by this point, audiences could be excused for literally losing the plot.

We're heading towards the resolution, however, and, with only a brief confusion around Cesario not realising he/she is supposed to be married to Olivia, all is soon revealed. Brother and sister are reunited, Olivia loves Sebastian, and Orsino (conveniently) loves Viola. Everyone is happy. Except Malvolio.

## IN A NUTSHELL

Gender swaps, mistaken identity and suspension of disbelief on the road to love.

## OTHER NOTABLE CHARACTERS

Feste, wiser than the average Shakespearean fool. And Maria, Olivia's serving woman, who ends up with Sir Toby.

## BODY COUNT

Although Olivia is in mourning at the beginning, Viola believes Sebastian dead and Orsino is frequently miserable as death, there are no actual deaths in the play.

## DID YOU KNOW?

❖ On the Elizabethan stage, Viola would have been played by a boy pretending to be a girl pretending to be a boy. Evidently there was no greater hilarity to be found in sixteenth-century London.

❖ The film *Shakespeare in Love* suggests a backstory to the writing of *Twelfth Night*, based on a sad ending to Shakespeare's love affair with Lady Viola de Lesseps, who dressed as a boy in order to act on stage.

❖ The full title of the play in the First Folio is *Twelfth Night, or What You Will*.

❖ The enjoyable Trevor Nunn-directed film of *Twelfth Night* (1996) with Imogen Stubbs also stars Mel Smith and Richard E. Grant as Sir Toby and Sir Andrew: roles they were born to.

❖ Graham Greene described *Twelfth Night* as Shakespeare's 'most perfect play'.

 QUOTABLE LINES

*'If music be the food of love, play on.'*

*'Some are born great, some achieve greatness, and some have greatness thrust upon 'em.'*

*'Better a witty fool than a foolish wit.'*

*'Thus the whirligig of time
brings in his revenges.'*

*'I'll be revenged on the whole pack of you.'*
**(POOR MALVOLIO.)**

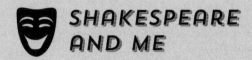

## SHAKESPEARE AND ME

*Charles Nicholl is an author and honorary professor of English at Sussex University. His books include* The Lodger: Shakespeare on Silver Street *and* The Reckoning: The Murder of Christopher Marlowe.

### What was your switch-on moment?

My teacher, Joe Bain, an erudite man, taught me *Othello* for A level. He showed me that a Shakespeare play is a tremendously complex mechanism. The other influence was Anthony Burgess's potboiler of a biography. That book brought alive the whole period, with details of Marlowe's knife fights and Robert Greene dining on pickled herring. It wasn't William Shakespeare on a pedestal, but the man out in the streets of the 1590s. I came of age in the sixties and saw parallels between the two times: the fast change, the young writer as a rock 'n' roll character...

**Which is your favourite of Shakespeare's plays?**

*Twelfth Night*. It's so intricate, subtle and teasing. It's a topsy-turvy world, with people cross-dressing, or impersonating someone else, and it's funny and sad. It has a melancholy, complex clown in Feste, and some really funny turns, like Malvolio. It's just a magical play.

**Tell us about the most memorable performance you've seen.**

Albert Finney as Hamlet, the opening performance at the Lyttelton Theatre in 1976. I don't know if he's considered a great Hamlet; I remember it being very loud, and they performed the whole thing with no cuts. But it was incredible seeing such an icon of sixties cinema on stage. And (a left-field choice) Charlie Drake as Touchstone in *As You Like It* at Ludlow Castle! He was very charismatic on stage, a childhood hero I associated with telly.

**Which Shakespeare character would you most like to meet?**

It's got to be Hamlet. Who wouldn't want to meet him? I'd love to ask him lots of questions. In many ways he's such a sympathetic character, but also a neurotic young man, slightly unsettling, full of complications. But always that tremendous spark of wit.

# THE TWO GENTLEMEN OF VERONA

This is generally considered to be Shakespeare's first play. Many of its themes were to become favourites: cross-dressing, tests of friendship, interfering parents, the daft behaviour of people in love, and women being oddly tolerant of the abuse meted out by their undeserving men. But he handled many of these ideas better in later plays.

## PLOT

Valentine and Proteus are BFFs who are sadly saying goodbye to each other. Valentine is off to travel the world, while Proteus is staying in Verona because he's in love with a lass called Julia. But their separation isn't long, for Proteus's father Antonio soon sends him to join Valentine in Milan. Proteus and Julia exchange rings and promises of fidelity.

At the Duke of Milan's court, Proteus finds that his old mucker Valentine is in love with Silvia, the Duke's daughter. Proteus instantly falls in love with her too, sending all thoughts of friendship and Julia out of the window, and caddishly tells the Duke that Valentine and Silvia are planning to elope. Valentine is banished, though Proteus doesn't do too well with Silvia, as she reminds him of his vows to Julia. That very woman, meanwhile, has turned up in Milan disguised as a man, planning an emotional reunion with Proteus. Unfortunately she's just in time to catch him (and Thurio, another suitor) wooing Silvia.

Meanwhile, the banished Valentine has been sort-of-kidnapped by a group of aristocratic outlaws who force him to lead them. Silvia and her friend Sir Eglamour set off to find

Valentine, and escape her father's insistence that she marry Thurio. However, she's captured by the outlaws (Sir Eglamour runs away). Thurio reveals his cowardice, but Proteus rescues Silvia from the outlaws. However, he then tries to rape her when she refuses to give in to him. Valentine appears in time to prevent this, and gives Proteus a hard time for his treachery. But as soon as Proteus apologises, Valentine forgives him and, bizarrely, offers him Silvia as a token of their friendship. Hey, wait up, fellas! She's not yours to give. Anyway, Julia, disguised as a page called Sebastian, faints on the spot, and her true identity is revealed. Proteus realises he loves her after all, the Duke agrees that Valentine can marry Silvia, and a double wedding is arranged. The Duke also pardons the outlaws.

## IN A NUTSHELL

Young men stick together despite at least one of them being an absolute rotter, and patient women eventually get the men they wanted all along.

## OTHER NOTABLE CHARACTERS

The comic double act of Lance, Proteus's servant, and Crab, his dog; the latter described by Stanley Wells as 'the most scene-stealing non-speaking role in the canon'.

## DID YOU KNOW?

- ❖ *The Two Gentlemen of Verona* has the smallest cast of all the plays.

- ❖ In the film *Shakespeare in Love*, Queen Elizabeth attends a performance of *Gentlemen*. She's highly amused at the antics of Crab the dog, but falls asleep later. Theatre impresario Philip Henslowe (played by Geoffrey Rush) keeps insisting that what audiences want is a funny play, with a dog.

- ❖ The real-life Shakespeare took no notice; this is his only play with a canine cast member.

- ❖ The song 'Who Is Silvia?' has been adapted by, amongst others, Schubert and Steve Winwood.

- ❖ George Eliot said she was 'disgusted' by the scene in which Valentine offers to give Silvia to Proteus. Some suggest that Valentine is offering to give Proteus all the *love* he would give to Silvia rather than the woman herself. Hmm. The jury's out.

 QUOTABLE LINES

'O, *how this spring of love resembleth The uncertain glory of an April day.*'

'*That man that hath a tongue I say is no man If with his tongue he cannot win a woman.*'

*'Who is Silvia? What is she,
That all our swains commend her?'*

*'O heaven, were man
But constant, he were perfect.'*

# THE TWO NOBLE KINSMEN

*The Two Noble Kinsmen* was missing from the First Folio but is now generally accepted as Shakespeare's final play, a collaboration between him and John Fletcher. It's not as good a swansong as the play previously considered his last, *The Tempest*, though, as author Andrew Dickson says of the play's closing lines, 'as a conclusion to his career these halting words... are infinitely more painful than anything voiced by Prospero'.

## PLOT

Cousins Palamon and Arcite are captured while fighting against Athens. In prison, they both fall in love with Emilia, sister of Hippolyta (wife of Theseus, Duke of Athens). The cousins' previously harmonious friendship is replaced by a jealous rivalry. Theseus sets Arcite free, though he banishes him. Palamon, meanwhile, is stuck in jail. But the jailer's nameless daughter falls in love with him and helps him escape. Arcite, who has returned in disguise and become Emilia's servant, stumbles upon Palamon in the forest, and they fight over Emilia. Theseus tries to banish them both, but they say they prefer death to losing Emilia. She, for her part, won't choose between them. Oh, these annoying young people! The presumably exasperated Theseus says that in that case, the two men will fight in a jousting competition. The winner will get Emilia's hand, and the loser will lose his head.

Meanwhile, the jailer's daughter goes mad for the love of Palamon, and dances crazily in the forest. Her former suitor ('the Wooer') pretends to be Palamon, and gradually she comes to her senses.

The jousting contest takes place noisily off stage. Arcite wins, and Palamon is set to be executed. But then Arcite is thrown from his horse, and fatally injured. Before he dies, he gives Emilia to Palamon.

## IN A NUTSHELL

Two cousins claim eternal friendship, then fall out over a girl. The one who wins her dies, so the other triumphs.

## OTHER NOTABLE CHARACTERS

The Doctor, who advises on treatment for the jailer's daughter's madness.

## BODY COUNT

Arcite, right at the end ('One kiss from fair Emilia: 'Tis done: Take her: I die.')

And at the beginning, the war the cousins fight in is triggered by the killing of three kings by Creon of Thebes (not seen on stage).

## DID YOU KNOW?

❖ *The Two Noble Kinsmen* wasn't considered to be part of Shakespeare's canon until the nineteenth century.

❖ The plot is based on a story by Chaucer (*The Knight's Tale*), a fact mentioned in the prologue to the play.

❖ Hippolyta and Theseus are characters in *A Midsummer Night's Dream* too, which is also partly based on *The Knight's Tale*.

❖ Scholars have proposed that Shakespeare wrote Act 1, two scenes in Act 3 and three in Act 5.

 QUOTABLE LINES

*'What things you make of us! For what we lack
We laugh, for what we have, are sorry; still
Are children in some kind. Let us be thankful
For that which is, and with you leave dispute
That are above our question.'*
(MORE OR LESS THE LAST WORDS
IN THE PLAY, OTHER THAN THE EPILOGUE;
RECKONED TO BE SHAKESPEARE'S, AND
THUS PERHAPS THE LAST WORDS HE WROTE.)

*'Men are mad things.'*

*'To marry him is hopeless,
To be his whore is witless.'*

'This world's a city full of straying streets,
And death's the market-place where each one meets.'

# THE WINTER'S TALE

*The Winter's Tale* is one of Shakespeare's last plays, probably written around 1609. It's yet another problem play, combining intense psychological drama with a smattering of comedy. For much of the action it mirrors the intensity of *Othello*, another play about jealousy, then it goes a bit mystical and fairy-tale-like towards the end. Alex Bledsoe, who based his novel *He Drank, And Saw the Spider* on the play, says of *The Winter's Tale*, 'This is no simple love story, or revenge tale. This one is just plain nuts.'

## PLOT

The Sicilian King, Leontes, becomes convinced that his pregnant wife, Hermione, has been unfaithful with their friend Polixenes. Leontes's jealousy gets so out of hand that he instructs his servant, Camillo, to poison Polixenes. But Camillo warns Polixenes and they both leg it to Bohemia, Polixenes's kingdom.

Poor Hermione is left to face the music. The crazed Leontes claims that the baby she's carrying isn't his and puts her in prison, where she gives birth to a daughter. Leontes instructs Lord Antigonus to abandon the baby far away. Antigonus takes her to good old Bohemia, where alas he's killed by a bear, and the baby girl is taken in by a shepherd. Meanwhile, the Delphic oracle consulted by Leontes proclaims that he was barking up the wrong tree and that, of course, his wife is faithful. Their son Mamillius dies from sorrow at his mother's imprisonment (and presumably his father's craziness), and hearing this, Hermione swoons clean away. It seems that she too has died. Leontes finally comes to his senses, rather too late, and spends the next 16 years mourning his wife, dead son and banished daughter.

That same daughter, Perdita, grows up happily as a shepherd's daughter. When she's 16, King Polixenes's son, Florizel, falls in love with her. They run away to Sicily, where Perdita is revealed as Hermione and Leontes's daughter. Paulina, Antigonus's widow, unveils a statue of Hermione. Leontes is grief-stricken all over again as he sees his poor wife's image – but then the statue moves, for it's the real Hermione, who has been living as a hermit (though some directors interpret her unexplained reappearance as a resurrection from the dead). Perdita and Florizel get together, Hermione and Leontes are reunited, Paulina finds love with Camillo, and it's all happy ever after. Apart from poor Mamillius and Antigonus.

## IN A NUTSHELL

King wrecks his family's life with his jealousy. And someone gets chased by a bear.

## OTHER NOTABLE CHARACTERS

Autolycus, a con man – often played by comic actors (Ron Moody and Jim Dale both took the part in the 1960s) – isn't essential to the plot but is one of the more prominent characters in the second half of the play, and has ten more speeches than Polixenes.

## BODY COUNT

Mamillius; Antigonus (presumably); and possibly Hermione, depending on how you interpret things, but anyway she's resurrected at the end.

### DID YOU KNOW?

❖ *The Winter's Tale* contains the most famous stage direction in all theatre: '*Exit, pursued by a bear.*' Unlike Leonardo DiCaprio's character in *The Revenant*, we don't see Antigonus being mauled by the beast, but as we never hear from him again, we must assume he's dead.

❖ Either this play or Ben Jonson's *The Alchemist* contains the first public airing of the word 'dildo'. (It's not clear which one was written first.) In *The Winter's Tale*, it comes up, as it were, when a naive servant doesn't realise it's a rude thing to talk about.

❖ To create *The Winter's Tale* Shakespeare reworked a popular novella called *Pandosto*, written by his old rival Robert Greene, the one who described young Shakespeare as an 'upstart crow'.

❖ Judi Dench's astonishing career can be judged by the fact that she played both Hermione in a 1969 RSC production and Paulina in Kenneth Branagh's production in 2015.

❖ The second-longest scene in all Shakespeare is the 'sheep-shearing scene' (Act 4, Scene 4), in which Perdita and Florizel express their love for each other. Only *Love's Labour's Lost* has a longer scene.

## QUOTABLE LINES

*'Exit, pursued by a bear.'*
**(STAGE DIRECTION.)**

*'But to be paddling palms and pinching fingers,*
*As now they are, and making practised smiles*
*As in a looking-glass.'*
**(LEONTES IS SUSPICIOUS ABOUT HIS FRIEND**
**AND WIFE TOGETHER.)**

*'A snapper-up of unconsidered trifles.'*

*'Daffodils,*
*That come before the swallow dares, and take*
*The winds of March with beauty.'*

*'A sad tale's best for winter.'*

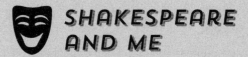

# SHAKESPEARE AND ME

*Vincent Adams has been a teacher and Theatre in Education practitioner, and has worked with students on many Shakespearean extracts and plays. He's played various roles, and directed* The Comedy of Errors, The Tempest *and* The Merry Wives of Windsor.

## What was your switch-on moment?

Shakespeare wrote plays, not exam papers, and I only began to enjoy it when I started to act it out. Forming the sounds of Shakespeare makes you rethink language, bringing old words and current meaning together. On a good night, the audience may even understand you. My first attempt was as a callow, teenaged Malvolio. Playing the box-tree scene was a turning point.

## Which is your favourite of Shakespeare's plays?

*The Winter's Tale* is my current favourite. It's one of those weird, adult fairy-tale plays that defies belief with such gravity that you go along with it. It's brittle and heartbreaking but also manages to pack in the Delphic oracle, some country dancing and a ravenous bear. I also have huge admiration for the craftsmanship of *The Comedy of Errors*: there isn't an ounce of fat on the bone and the situations work as well today as they ever did.

## Tell us about the most memorable production you've seen?

Andrew Jarvis and Michael Pennington, vicious and hilarious by turns in the English Shakespeare Company's *Richard III*; the puppet Ariel in the BBC's stop-frame animated *Tempest* outdoing mere mortal actors by actually flying and vanishing; Steven Berkoff running up all the stairs in Elsinore in his brilliantly clever *Shakespeare's Villains*; Peter Brook's absorbing *Hamlet* in 90 minutes with just some cushions and an orange rug.

## Which Shakespeare character have you most enjoyed playing?

Polonius. I've spent many hours of my life listening to other people going on a bit, and it was lovely to get my own back and insist that everyone needed to know exactly why borrowing dulls the edge of husbandry. It's extraordinary to see how a man with the best intentions can fail so badly at fatherhood. I also mastered the art of dying behind an arras without concussing myself on the adjacent flat.

## How would you persuade somebody to give Shakespeare a chance?

Get them to act a bit or read it out loud with you, like Alan Bennett's King George III reading *King Lear* with his doctor. Then talk about it, try to understand it and then read it again. After all, you can never have too much of a good thing.

## CHAPTER FOUR
# THE HISTORIES

Sure, they all deal with a historical figure and setting, but this doesn't fully describe the history plays: some are comic; some tragic; most are a mixture of both. What they have in common is that they all concern events in *English* history. Other plays obviously have historical content (e.g. the Roman ones, such as *Julius Caesar*) but are mostly classed as tragedies.

Unlike the other chapters dealing with the comedies and tragedies, I've put the history plays into a chronological order. Thus they run from *King John*, set around 1200, to the more contemporary (at least for Shakespeare's audience) *Henry VIII*, set in the 1530s.

## *KING JOHN*

Set around 200 years before Shakespeare's better-known sequence of history plays, *King John* nonetheless covers many similar themes: political manoeuvrings, wars of royal succession and the question of whether the King is up to the job. Despite the relative obscurity of the play, the historical King John was one of

England's most significant monarchs, and the play takes in some of his highlights (or perhaps lowlights).

## PLOT

Richard the Lionheart (Richard I) has no legitimate children and, on his death, the crown has passed to his little brother John. However, the French are backing Arthur, nephew of John and Richard, and soon, inevitably, we're heading for war.

The French and English armies confront each other at the town of Angers. Even the mothers get involved, with Eleanor (John's mum) and Constance (Arthur's) trading insults. The citizens of Angers hedge their bets, saying that the battle will determine whether the King should be John or Arthur. This clever strategy backfires when, following an inconclusive battle, it's suggested that the armies join forces to attack the town. The citizens avoid apocalypse by cleverly proposing a marriage alliance between England and France. The French Dauphin, Louis, marries John's daughter, and the French receive a chunk of territory. In return John gets French support for his claim to the throne of England. Constance is, to say the least, rather put out.

It turns out to be a pyrrhic victory for John. Cardinal Pandolf, an ambassador from the Pope, arrives, displeased that John has appointed an archbishop without approval from Rome. The consequence is excommunication for John, followed by the French King reneging on a treaty.

War is on again, and Arthur is captured by the English. John vacillates over killing him; Arthur eventually dies falling off a castle wall. Whether this is suicide or a bungled escape is unclear, but John is blamed by his nobles, who start siding with the French. The advantage shifts England's way when French reinforcements are shipwrecked, but it's too late for John, who, taking refuge in a monastery, is poisoned by a monk. Pandolf negotiates a treaty to stop a final battle, and the English nobles swear allegiance to John's son, Henry III.

## IN A NUTSHELL

King John mismanages a war with France and botches relations with the Catholic Church. He loses a large slice of his kingdom and is killed by a member of the clergy.

## OTHER NOTABLE CHARACTERS

Though Richard I had no legitimate children, we discover an illegitimate one, Philip 'Bastard' Falconbridge, early in the play. 'Bastard' is, depending on your perspective, either a hero or, in fact, a complete bastard. He's the one who suggests the armies unite to punish the citizens of Angers. He serves John loyally, though.

## BODY COUNT

'Bastard' beheads the Duke of Austria, who may have killed his father; Arthur has his ambiguous fall; and John is poisoned. The deaths of nameless soldiers don't really register.

## DID YOU KNOW?

❖ *King John* was the first Shakespeare play to be filmed, or at least to have one scene filmed: in 1899, Herbert Beerbohm Tree made a short silent movie of the King's death scene.

❖ Its heyday was the nineteenth century, when it was evidently one of Shakespeare's most popular plays.

❖ The biggest event of the real King John's career, the signing of Magna Carta, doesn't make it into the story.

## QUOTABLE LINES

*'Mad world, mad kings, mad composition!'*

*'Grief fills the room up of my absent child,*
*Lies in his bed, walks up and down with me,*
*Puts on his pretty looks, repeats his words,*
*Remembers me of all his gracious parts,*
*Stuffs out his vacant garments with his form;*
*Then have I reason to be fond of grief.*
*Fare you well. Had you such a loss as I,*
*I could give better comfort than you do.'*
(IT'S BEEN SPECULATED THAT THESE LINES, SPOKEN BY CONSTANCE WHEN SHE THINKS ARTHUR IS DEAD, RELATE TO THE DEATH OF SHAKESPEARE'S OWN SON, HAMNET.)

# EDWARD III

*Edward III* wasn't in the First Folio, and has spent much of its existence outside the Shakespearean canon. However, in the last 25 years, many academics have accepted that he had at least a hand in writing it, probably early on in his career in the 1590s. The bulk of the play is reckoned to have been penned by Thomas Kyd.

For historical context: Edward III was the son of Edward II, and the father of the Black Prince and John of Gaunt. He was succeeded by his grandson, Richard II (who has his own play). Edward III started all the unpleasantness with France that became the Hundred Years' War.

## PLOT

We open with Edward in full Plantagenet mode: asserting his claim to the throne of France, intimidating the cowardly Scots in the Borders and plotting adultery with the Countess of Salisbury. Her threats of suicide (how bad can he be?) remind him of his responsibilities, and glory on the fields of France beckons.

He's a tough egg, though. He refuses to help his son, the Black Prince, who is, in his turn, merciless against the foe at the Battle of Crécy. He gets a knighthood from Dad for his pains, then is despatched to Poitiers. Spurning offers of treaty, he triumphs over a larger French force, capturing their king.

In Calais, meanwhile, Edward is planning siege warfare. Calais expels six of its poorest people in the hope that this will appease the English, but Edward unexpectedly shows these people clemency, demanding Calais' six richest citizens instead. Edward also gets to capture the King of the Scots for good measure.

To give him his due, he spends some time mulling over the downside of war. But that's soon forgotten when he learns of the victory in Poitiers. Triumph seems so complete that you wonder how the war continued for the next century.

## IN A NUTSHELL

The English King and his son boss it in France.

## OTHER NOTABLE CHARACTERS

The Earl of Salisbury, a sort of Plantagenet Peter Mandelson, smoothing the way to Calais.

## BODY COUNT

At one point Edward thinks the Black Prince has been killed, but this turns out to be false.

Presumably a load of insignificant people are killed in battle.

### DID YOU KNOW?

*Edward III* takes a negative view of the Scots, who are depicted as cowardly and untrustworthy. While this may have gone down a storm in the 1590s, it would be reasonable to assume that ten years later, with the Scottish James I on the throne, it was less well received. As James I was also patron of the King's Men, one can't help wondering if Shakespeare may have been keen to distance himself from any connection to the play. Perhaps this is why it was absent from the First Folio.

## QUOTABLE LINES

There aren't really any. There are one or two nice bits, though, which might just have been written by the master.

> *'My eyes shall be my arrows, and my sighs*
> *Shall serve me as the vantage of the wind,*
> *To whirl away my sweetest artillery.*
> *Ah, but alas, she wins the sun of me,*
> *For that is she herself, and thence it comes*
> *That poets term the wanton warrior blind.*
> *But love hath eyes as judgement to his steps,*
> *Till too much lovèd glory dazzles them.'*

# RICHARD II

*Richard II* is the first (chronologically) of Shakespeare's series of plays known as the 'Henriad', which recounts the dynastic struggles of England before the accession of the Tudors. The others are the Henrys (the many parts of *IV* and *VI*) and *Richard III*. *Henry V* falls in the middle of the sequence but concentrates more on England's ongoing war with France.

## PLOT

The action takes place in the twilight of possibly the worst Plantagenet king. Setting high taxes, annoying the barons, offing his enemies – there are no depths to which Richard II won't stoop. We kick off with his adjudication of a duel to the death between his cousin Henry Bolingbroke (sometimes known by his nickname, Harry) and Thomas Mowbray (thought to have murdered the Duke of Gloucester). Richard calls the contest off and exiles the protagonists, though in the case of Bolingbroke this proves a big mistake. Richard's uncle, John of Gaunt (the Duke of Lancaster and Henry's dad), and many others suspect Richard to have been complicit in Gloucester's murder. Throw in a rebellion in Ireland and Richard couldn't be less popular.

Gaunt's eloquent death speech moves Richard not a jot and, as soon as the old man expires, his estates are confiscated to give to royal favourites. Ignoring rumours that Bolingbroke may return (he's Gaunt's heir, after all), Richard heads for Ireland to sort out the rebels. Bolingbroke, seeing his chance, returns with an army and the people rally to his cause. This includes not only getting back what's his, but taking the crown itself.

But Bolingbroke is a reluctant usurper, despite having the upper hand. Richard is still the legitimate king when all's said and done. Richard abdicates and then, in his wretched state, turns out to be rather more endearing than anyone expected. Henry is crowned Henry IV, Richard is imprisoned, plots are foiled and a retainer eventually kills Richard, believing that Henry has ordered it. Neither we, nor indeed Henry, seem quite clear what his real intentions were. With the victor heading for a pilgrimage to the Holy Land, and full of uncertainty and remorse, the stage is set for *Henry IV, Part I*.

## IN A NUTSHELL

Is being the rightful king enough, even if you're an incompetent tyrant?

## OTHER NOTABLE CHARACTERS

Henry 'Harry Hotspur' Percy, who takes centre stage in *Henry IV*.

## BODY COUNT

An awful lot of banishment goes on but comparatively few deaths. Several of the Irish presumably get killed off stage, but battle in England is prevented. Henry avoids a lethal duel and assassination, John of Gaunt dies of old age and Richard is stabbed to death.

## DID YOU KNOW?

❖ It was *Richard II* that nearly got the Chamberlain's Men into terrible trouble with the Queen when, in 1601, they performed it at the request and payment of the Earl of Essex's supporters. It turned out that Essex was using this play – about the overthrow of a king – as a subtle call to arms for rebellion. Essex lost his head for the plot, but Shakespeare and his colleagues were excused for their unwitting role in events.

❖ The historical Richard II was king at the time of the Peasants' Revolt, a rebellion about taxes in 1381. Aged only 14, he met the rebels at Smithfield near London and agreed to most of their demands. That seems to have been a ruse, however, and with the extra time gained he gathered an army and defeated the uprising. It was probably the high point of his reign, during which he was deposed twice.

 QUOTABLE LINES

*'This royal throne of kings, this sceptred isle,*
*This earth of majesty, this seat of Mars,*
*This other Eden, demi-paradise,*
*This fortress built by nature for herself*
*Against infection and the hand of war,*
*This happy breed of men, this little world,*
*This precious stone set in the silver sea,*
*Which serves it in the office of a wall,*
*Or as a moat defensive to a house*
*Against the envy of less happier lands;*
*This blessèd plot, this earth, this realm, this England.'*
**(JOHN OF GAUNT IN PATRIOTIC MOOD.)**

*'For God's sake, let us sit upon the ground,*
*And tell sad stories of the death of kings.'*

# HENRY IV
# (PARTS I AND II)

'Uneasy lies the head that wears a crown,' says Henry Bolingbroke, who becomes King Henry IV. He doesn't say this till *Part II*, but the sentiment underlies the whole cycle of Shakespeare's history plays, from the deposition of Richard II, set in the late 1390s, to Richard III's cry for equine assistance at Bosworth Field, set more than 80 years later. *Henry IV Part I* follows directly on from events at the end of *Richard II*.

## PLOTS

### Part I

Henry Bolingbroke is now King Henry IV. He has only just seized the throne from his cousin, Richard II, and already he has problems. Having set a precedent by usurping the legitimate line of succession, Henry has encouraged others to fancy their chances. For instance, the rebellious Prince Owain Glyndŵr is becoming uppity in Wales, and has imprisoned the English Earl of Mortimer. The Scots are being put in their place, however, by the dashing young Sir Henry 'Hotspur' Percy, son of the Earl of Northumberland. Nonetheless, this only deepens the King's gloom, because his own son, Prince Hal, spends his time carousing in the taverns of Eastcheap, hanging out with lowlifes like Sir John Falstaff, dabbling in petty crime and generally scrubbing up badly as heir to the throne.

Things take a turn for the worse when Henry refuses to pay the ransom for Mortimer, and Hotspur (Mortimer's brother-in-law) starts to plot rebellion. Mortimer is soon in league with Glyndŵr, the Percy family and the Scots. Battle is imminent. It's the perfect chance for Hal to prove himself, so what else would he do but ask Falstaff to take command of a group of foot soldiers and generally provide comic relief? (Falstaff remains in character by taking bribes from men who want to avoid military service.)

The climax comes with Hal rescuing his father in battle and going mano-a-mano with Hotspur (this town ain't big enough, etc.). Hal kills Hotspur, the rebels are temporarily routed and Falstaff, thought to be dead, turns out to be just pretending (which is a sensible way to avoid getting really dead).

## Part II

Despite following straight on from *Part I* (we come in when Northumberland is about to find out that his son, Hotspur, is dead), *Part II* offers a very different atmosphere. Instead of action and glory, a pall hangs over the King and court.

Rebellion against Henry's rule continues. Even the Archbishop of York is mustering forces, but the clergy did that kind of thing in the fifteenth century. After his triumph in *Part I*, Prince Hal is more involved in court life, though he still spends too much time in his old seamy haunts for the King's liking. But he is less pally with Sir John Falstaff, who's in trouble with the Lord Chief Justice because of his bad influence on the Prince. One of the few scenes with Falstaff and Hal involves the Prince overhearing Falstaff complaining about him. Falstaff attempts to explain it away but Hal is summoned to court before things are settled.

We don't see much of King Henry but it's clear that – what with the rebellion gathering force again, a wayward son and the weight of being a usurper – he's feeling the pressure. Falstaff joins up once more and leads an army of yokels for the royal forces.

The rebellion is defeated largely due to the machinations of Prince John, Hal's brother. He promises to hear the rebels' complaints then double-crosses them. King Henry is by now in such a state that even news of victory is too much for him to handle and he collapses. Everyone assumes he's dead, and Hal is a little too quick to pick up the crown, but then Henry wakes up. Presumably there's a small moment of mutual surprise, then the two are reconciled, before Henry does die. For real this time.

Falstaff rushes to London, eager to be the friend and mentor of the new King Henry V. Hal/Henry V is having none of it and, in one of the most poignant scenes in Shakespeare, repudiates his old life and old friends ('I know thee not, old man'). On the plus side, now we're all set for the Battle of Agincourt and the zenith of English glory.

## IN A NUTSHELL

Being king doesn't quite work out like Henry IV hoped. Rebellion is staved off when his wastrel son gets his act together and saves the day.

## OTHER NOTABLE CHARACTERS

Mistress Quickly, saucy wench, keeper of the Boar's Head Tavern and queen of the double entendre. She's annoyed with Falstaff for playing fast and loose with her heart. Doll Tearsheet, a prostitute who canoodles with Falstaff and is last seen heavily pregnant. Justices Shallow and Silence, old men addicted to reminiscence.

## BODY COUNT

Hotspur is the big one. Rebels Thomas Percy (the Earl of Worcester) and Sir Richard Vernon are, not without a certain pleasure on Henry's part, sentenced to death at the end of *Part I*. King Henry dies at the end of *Part II*, clearing the way for his son to ascend to the throne.

---

### DID YOU KNOW?

❖ *Henry IV, Part I* was apparently the most commercially successful of the plays in Shakespeare's lifetime.

❖ It's thought that the character of Falstaff was written for Will Kemp, the actor in the Lord Chamberlain's Men who was known for his comic roles. Kemp apparently left the company in the late 1590s and died in poverty a few years later.

❖ *Part I* is the more popular of the two plays; *Part II* is rarely produced without it. Sometimes the same actor plays Hal/Henry through to the end of *Henry V*, such as in the BBC's *The Hollow Crown* (2012), with Tom Hiddleston going all the way from the Boar's Head to Agincourt.

❖ Gus Van Sant's 1991 film *My Own Private Idaho*, with Keanu Reeves, is loosely based on the *Henry IV* plays.

❖ The character of Falstaff has always been one of Shakespeare's most popular creations – so much so that he reappears in *The Merry Wives of Windsor*, set 200 years after the reign of Henry IV.

##  QUOTABLE LINES

### PART I
*'In those holy fields*
*Over whose acres walked those blessèd feet*
*Which fourteen hundred years ago were nailed,*
*For our advantage, on the bitter cross.'*

*'Hal, if I tell thee a lie, spit in my face, call me horse.'*

### PART II
*'I am not only witty in myself,*
*but the cause that wit is in other men.'*

*'Uneasy lies the head that wears a crown.'*

*'Thy wish was father, Harry, to that thought.'*

*'I know thee not, old man. Fall to thy prayers.*
*How ill white hairs becomes a fool and jester!'*

# SHAKESPEARE AND ME

*Rob Howell is a freelance set and costume designer. He worked at the RSC in the early 1990s.*

### What was your switch-on moment?

I trained in theatre design at Birmingham, and as we were just up the road from Stratford, we went quite often to see shows at the RSC. I remember very clearly Maria Björnson's design for *The Tempest*. The scene where the shipwreck changed to the island was breathtaking. When I left college I became the resident design assistant at the RSC for two and a half years. It was a very exciting time, and an unbelievable opportunity to see how a cautious or bold design affected a production.

### Which is your favourite of Shakespeare's plays?

Can I have two? Probably the *Henry IV*s, *Parts I* and *II*. Such expanse and detail!

### Tell us about the most memorable performance you've seen.

Robert Stephens as Falstaff in *Henry IV* for the RSC (1993). It was pretty special. He had such a command of the stage, the auditorium and the words. It was all the best bits of what some would say is an 'old-school' performance.

> **Which Shakespeare character would you most like to meet?**
>
> Well, Caliban would be fun!

# HENRY V

In *Henry V* we catch up with the wild Prince Hal (of *Henry IV Parts I* and *II*), now King himself and on the verge of becoming England's greatest military leader.

## PLOT

Trying to live down his rowdy past with Falstaff and other ne'er-do-wells, the young King Henry lays claim, as any red-blooded Plantagenet would, to the throne of France. Henry's demands for his rights produces a condescending gift of tennis balls from the French Dauphin. The economic benefits of Wimbledon being some way in the future, the King is insulted. As this is the medieval period, insult can only lead to one thing.

From the nobles and clergy to Henry's old lowlife associates (Pistol, Nim and Bardolph), the country prepares for war. It becomes clear that Henry is no longer the feckless Prince Hal; he shows his mettle with a swift execution of some advisers found plotting to kill him, and with the conquest of the port of Harfleur. For an encore, he has Bardolph hanged for a trivial crime. By this point you know he really means business.

More than ruthlessness, or even the famed English longbows, Henry's main asset is being a top-notch motivational speaker.

The French are very slow to recognise the trouble they're in – all perhaps except Catherine, the French King's daughter, who squeezes in a few English lessons in anticipation of becoming a trophy wife in the Home Counties.

The French still have an overwhelming numerical advantage over the English ragtag and bobtail Army, and anticipate they'll handily sort them out at Agincourt. Henry, rejecting invitations to surrender, walks through the English camp in disguise, talking to the common soldiers and gathering material for one of the greatest speeches in Shakespeare, the 'St Crispin's Day' speech. After the English Army have been roused by rhetoric, the French don't stand a chance. Following their surrender, Henry marries Catherine (she saw it coming), and becomes heir to the French throne. The Hundred Years' War looks to be over after a mere 68 years. Honestly, though! The clue was in the name (the war is taken up again in the next play, *Henry VI, Part I*).

## IN A NUTSHELL

France beaten by an English team captained by a warrior-king with a stunning line in speech-making.

## OTHER NOTABLE CHARACTERS

The Duke of Exeter, Henry's uncle. Close your eyes and think of Brian Blessed roaring.

## BODY COUNT

High – unsurprisingly, given this is a war epic. Notable deaths include Sir John Falstaff (which we hear about rather than see); Bardolph; and the three assassination plotters (the Earl of Cambridge, Lord Scrope and Sir Thomas Grey).

### DID YOU KNOW?

❖ The 'wooden O' mentioned in the opening speech of the play has long been assumed to refer to the newly built Globe of 1599. However, Shakespearean scholar James Shapiro believes the evidence favours a first production at the Curtain Theatre instead.

❖ The ferocious English longbows were the super-weapon of their time. They were difficult to master, requiring skill and great physical strength. Edward III (a few decades before Henry) had decreed that every Englishman should practise archery. The bowmen released a powerful hail of arrows on their foes.

❖ *Henry V* is one of the few Shakespeare plays whose writing can be precisely dated, because it refers to a specific historical event: the anticipated triumphant return from Ireland of the Earl of Essex. He returned in disgrace in late 1599, so the play must have been written in early 1599, when it was still assumed that he'd be coming home in glory.

##  QUOTABLE LINES

'Can this cock-pit hold
The vasty fields of France?'

'Even at the turning o' the tide.'

'As cold as any stone.'

'From this day to the ending of the world,
But we in it shall be rememberèd;
We few, we happy few, we band of brothers.'

'For he today that sheds his blood with me
Shall be my brother.'

'And gentlemen in England now abed
Shall think themselves accursed they were not here,
And hold their manhoods cheap whiles any speaks
That fought with us upon Saint Crispin's day.'

'Once more unto the breach, dear friends, once more,
Or close the wall up with our English dead.'

'The game's afoot.
Follow your spirit, and upon this charge
Cry, "God for Harry! England and Saint George!"'

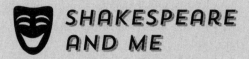

# SHAKESPEARE AND ME

*Steven Gauge is the author of* My Life as a Hooker, *his story of taking up rugby at the age of 35. By day he's a political and PR consultant based in Westminster. He was third sword-bearer in a student production of* Julius Caesar *in the 1980s.*

## What was your switch-on moment?

In the sixth form, a new English teacher took a group of us to Bankside, now the home of the Globe but then a grubby, slightly smelly confusion of alleyways and warehouses. We were treated to an alcoholic drink, and visited the museum where plans to resurrect the Globe were on display. I got the sense that Shakespeare was rooted in the rough and ready side of London, as much about the groundlings as the elites in the wooden seats. Shakespeare is for me part of my South London heritage, the aromas of street markets and the dirt under my fingernails.

## Which is your favourite of Shakespeare's plays?

*Henry V* does it every time for me. It mines the rich comedy vein of the national stereotypes that unite in this little kingdom, says more about leadership than a million MBAs and it has some fun with our friends the French. Just thinking now about those stirring speeches on the eve of battle gets the hairs on the back of my neck standing up to attention.

**Tell us about the most memorable performance you've seen.**

I will never forget the all-female performance of *Henry V* by a group of Durham University students. Not only did these young women find new ways of exploring the traditional male themes of war and valour but the most memorable moment was seeing my daughter as Mistress Quickly locking tonsils in a full-on passionate embrace with the girl who was playing Pistol. It was a bit of a shock for her old dad. She carried it off impeccably but we've never spoken of it again.

**Which Shakespeare character would you most like to meet?**

I'd like to invite Sir John Falstaff for a few beers and some banter at my rugby club. We might even persuade him to run out for the 4th XV, where he'd add a bit of ballast to the scrum.

**How would you persuade somebody to give Shakespeare a chance?**

Go to Stratford and see Shakespeare done by the best in the business. The RSC actors know how to bring the language alive and you can enjoy it without having to work hard.

# HENRY VI
# (PARTS I, II AND III)

Believed to be amongst Shakespeare's earliest produced plays, the three parts of *Henry VI* depict the Wars of the Roses, the fifteenth-century wars of English succession. While not frequently performed today, it may be that the Henrys packed in the crowds in the 1590s. The chaotic events of the previous century would have had a special resonance, as Queen Elizabeth didn't have an obvious heir. The Plantagenets' successors, the Tudors and Stuarts, were Shakespeare's patrons, and he might have had an interest in providing an unflattering portrayal of the pre-Tudor period. Also, he was never one for letting humdrum reality get in the way of a good story.

## PLOTS

### Part I
Following the untimely death of Henry V, conqueror of France, England passes into the hands of child king Henry VI. The French stage a comeback, inspired by peasant girl Joan la Pucelle (Joan of Arc). Henry VI's reign then goes rapidly downhill with internecine fighting in England between the heirs of Henry IV (the House of Lancaster, including the current king) and the descendants of the previously deposed Richard II (the House of York, now led by Richard Plantagenet). The King annoys both factions, and makes heavy weather of it militarily in France. He ends up marrying a French princess, Margaret of Anjou, and gets a bad deal in his negotiations with the Gallic foe. Further trouble is inevitable.

## Part II

England is in uproar. Henry's forthcoming marriage and crappy terms from the French have led to demands for his removal. Even his wife is no comfort, as she's in cahoots with the Duke of Suffolk; they work together to kill Henry's uncle and protector, the Duke of Gloucester. Suffolk is rapidly exiled then killed at sea, but by then rebellion is building. This is nominally led by Jack Cade, a commoner, but is orchestrated by Richard of York, Henry's main challenger for the throne. Things come out in the open soon enough, and the Wars of the Roses are in full swing. Following defeat by Yorkists at St Albans, Henry and Margaret flee to London.

## Part III

Henry is forced into a compromise: he can retain the throne, but Richard becomes his heir rather than Henry's own son Edward. Queen Margaret is not so quiescent and fights on in the interests of the disinherited Edward. York breaks the deal, declares himself King and is promptly killed by Margaret's forces. Richard's son, rather confusingly also called Edward, is then proclaimed King (Edward IV). Henry ends up in the Tower of London. King Edward IV blackmails a noblewoman into marriage – evidently his being a king of dubious legitimacy is insufficiently appealing for her. The whole play ends in a bloody melee, with the Yorkists ultimately ascendant and Henry VI murdered in the Tower.

## IN A NUTSHELL

The later Plantagenet period is a right old mess, characterised by incompetence abroad and brutal factional warfare at home.

## OTHER NOTABLE CHARACTERS

Richard, Earl of Salisbury, later Duke of Gloucester, who's the son of Richard of York and the younger brother of Edward IV. As he makes very clear, all of those grand titles aren't enough for him. Richard apparently has a hunchback, which would have sealed his fate as a baddie for Elizabethan audiences. What happens to him can be seen in *Richard III*; keep an eye out for his tendency to murder anyone with a better claim to the throne than his own.

## BODY COUNT

Extremely high, as befits one of the more brutal periods in English history. Noteworthy deaths include Joan of Arc, burned at the stake in *Part I*.

Gloucester, Suffolk, a lot of sundry nobles and Jack Cade don't make it through *Part II*. Richard's son, the Earl of Rutland, pops up to be killed in *Part III*.

Other later deaths include Lancastrians the Earl of Warwick and his brother the Marquis of Montague. Edward (Henry's son) is executed and then, pulling a fast one, Richard (Richard of York's son) stabs Henry. There are probably more fatalities but it's hard to keep track.

## DID YOU KNOW?

❖ While Shakespeare portrayed Henry VI as a teen or young adult at the time of his father's death, the historical Henry was only nine months old when he became King of England and France, the youngest ever English ruler. (He's beaten to the equivalent title in France by John I, who became French King in 1316, the day he was born.)

❖ *Henry VI, Part I* is one of the many plays considered to be Shakespeare's weakest because of a likely collaboration (this one possibly with Thomas Nashe).

❖ *Henry VI, Part II* is regarded as the best of the trilogy (perhaps like *The Godfather Part II*). It has the largest cast in the entire canon: about 50 named parts, plus dozens of other servants, neighbours, soldiers, rebels, etc.

❖ *Henry VI, Part III* has the most battle scenes of any Shakespeare play.

## QUOTABLE LINES

### PART I

*'And here I prophesy: this brawl today,*
*Grown to this faction in the Temple garden,*
*Shall send, between the red rose and the white,*
*A thousand souls to death and deadly night.'*

'Done like a Frenchman – turn and turn again.'

'The first thing we do, let's kill all the lawyers.'

'Let them obey that knows not how to rule.'

'Why, what is pomp, rule, reign, but earth and dust?
And, live we how we can, yet die we must.'

'Would I were dead, if God's good will were so –
For what is in this world but grief and woe?'

# RICHARD III

The Henriad group of history plays comes to a triumphant conclusion with the story of the last Plantagenet ruler: the hunchbacked villain who will do anything for power. Thought to have been written in the early 1590s, this is perhaps the moment we see Shakespeare touching greatness for the first time. Richard III is evil, dishonest, boastful, captivating, hilarious and deadly: arguably Shakespeare's finest creation. Hamlet is 'the Dane' but Richard is 'the King'.

## PLOT

Following the overthrow of Henry VI, England is at peace and ruled by Edward IV of the House of York. Not everyone's happy, though: Edward's younger brother, Richard, for instance, who confides his discontent to the audience. He lusts for the throne and is bitter about his physical deformities. Woe betide anyone who gets in his way. First in the firing line is his brother George, Duke of Clarence, who's sent to the Tower after Richard convinces Edward that George is a danger.

Richard clearly lusts after lust too and, in a famous scene, woos Lady Anne (the daughter-in-law of Henry VI) right over Henry's coffin. This is creepy – especially as Richard was involved in the murder of Henry *and* his son, her husband – but also surprisingly successful. Though Anne will clearly be dumped when her purpose is served, Richard is a breathtakingly good liar. He's also superb at drawing us, the audience, in; at charming us, and making us complicit in his machinations, often against our will.

And what machinations they are. Richard has Clarence swiftly despatched, and the ailing King Edward dies soon after. Richard uses his position as Lord Protector, an ironic title if ever there was one, to launch an all-out purge against courtiers loyal to Edward's two sons. The two young Princes are conveyed to the Tower (their feisty banter with Richard doesn't save them), and Richard is quickly questioning their legitimacy and presenting himself as the true heir to the throne.

The young Princes are murdered, and for an encore the tireless Richard poisons Lady Anne to free himself up to pursue the Princes' sister, Elizabeth. However, rebellion is afoot in the kingdom, with Henry Tudor, Earl of Richmond, leading the agitators. Things begin to go badly for Richard, and he's roundly cursed by the women in his family, including his own mother, which doesn't help.

The final act follows Richard's attempt to stomp on the rebellion at Bosworth Field. Ghosts of his executed foes visit him the night before the decisive battle – never a good sign. It's probably no surprise therefore that, friendless and famously horseless, Richard is killed in combat with Richmond. Richmond becomes Henry VII, ushering in the Tudor era.

## IN A NUTSHELL

The most villainous of villains will do anything to gain the throne. He gets there but it's all downhill from then on.

## OTHER NOTABLE CHARACTERS

The Duke of Buckingham, Richard's henchman, who balks at killing the Princes in the Tower. Queen Margaret, whose husband and son were killed by Richard yet who is bravely willing to face him down.

## BODY COUNT

In this, as in so many other respects, *Richard III* is on an immense scale. The bodies pile up, though not literally in the manner of *Othello*: King Edward, the two Princes, their supporters (Earl Rivers, Lord Hastings, Lord Gray and Sir Thomas Vaughan, who are executed), Anne and Buckingham all die out of our sight. Richard dies on stage, and Clarence is stabbed in front of us then dragged off to be drowned in a vat of wine.

## DID YOU KNOW?

❖ 'It seems terribly unfair of Shakespeare to begin his play with such a famous speech,' said Antony Sher in *Year of the King*, the book he wrote about preparing for the role (the one I saw) in 1984, acknowledging ruefully just how many actors had been there before him.

❖ *Richard III* is the second-longest play after *Hamlet* in terms of the number of words, though measured by lines it comes in fourth. Richard himself has more than 300 speeches and is barely off stage, making the part an Everest for actors. Anecdote has it that Richard Burbage (the first man to play Richard) pinned Shakespeare against a wall and said words to the effect of 'do that to me again and I'll kill you'.

❖ Classic films include Laurence Olivier's definitive version from the 1950s; Al Pacino's documentary *Looking for Richard*; and Richard Dreyfuss's Oscar-winning turn as a struggling actor hamming up (and camping up) Richard in Neil Simon's *The Goodbye Girl*.

❖ The Richard III Society exists to try to correct the portrayal of Richard in Shakespeare's play. Unjustly maligned or not, you do wonder whether without Shakespeare's marvellous villain, the historical Richard, King for only a couple of years, would be remembered as anything more than a footnote. The discovery of Richard's body beneath a Leicester car park in 2012 confirmed that, while not definitively an 'evil hunchback', Richard did have a curved spine.

 QUOTABLE LINES

'Now is the winter of our discontent
Made glorious summer by this son of York.'

'I that am curtailed of this fair proportion,
Cheated of feature by dissembling nature,
Deformed, unfinished, sent before my time
Into this breathing world scarce half made up.'

'Was ever woman in this humour wooed?
Was ever woman in this humour won?'

'And thus I clothe my naked villainy
With odd old ends, stol'n forth of Holy Writ,
And seem a saint when most I play the devil.'

'And every tale condemns me for a villain.'

'So wise so young, they say, do never live long.'

'A horse! A horse! My kingdom for a horse!'

# HENRY VIII

Thought to be a late collaboration between Shakespeare and John Fletcher, *Henry VIII* revisits the themes of court machinations and royal succession anxieties of the earlier history plays. With an eye for significant events, the play is set at the time of Henry's divorce from Catherine of Aragon (Katherine in the play) in order to marry Anne Boleyn, one of the biggest turning points in English history. With an equal instinct for a big character, much of the story is focused on Cardinal Wolsey.

## PLOT

Henry VIII's court is at its stylish zenith. What with the Field of the Cloth of Gold (the Tudor equivalent of a glitzy peace conference), and hobnobbing with the French nobility, Cardinal Wolsey (Lord Chancellor and Archbishop of Canterbury) is feeling pretty pleased with himself. Of course, he has enemies, who regard him as a low-born social climber. He arranges for the arrest and trial of the Duke of Buckingham, the leading Wolsey-sceptic. Queen Katherine opposes Buckingham's arrest, a bad move as she's already on thin ice, what with King Henry becoming fascinated by Anne Bullen (Boleyn to you and me).

As Buckingham goes off to his execution, Wolsey's hostility to Katherine grows increasingly evident. Divorce proceedings begin, with Katherine putting up a robust defence and walking out. In the hiatus, Wolsey's opponents luck into a packet of letters showing that he's been advocating divorce to the King but opposing it in communications with the Pope. Wolsey is a busted flush, but this doesn't stop the divorce going through. Shortly afterwards, Anne is crowned Queen, and Katherine sickens and dies.

There's a bit more intrigue but the last act moves swiftly to the rejoicing over the birth of Henry and Anne's daughter, the future Queen Elizabeth I. Both Elizabeth and her successor were marked for glory – conveniently, given that King James I was by now on the throne.

## IN A NUTSHELL

King wants a new wife. His scheming official and his first wife are collateral damage.

## OTHER NOTABLE CHARACTERS

Thomas Cromwell, Wolsey's protégé, who later rises in royal favour. One of the most interesting people in the whole of English history – catch up with him in Hilary Mantel's *Wolf Hall*.

## BODY COUNT

Buckingham, jealous of Wolsey, pays the ultimate price. Katherine dies after a vision of dancing spirits.

## DID YOU KNOW?

❖ The most dramatic staging of *Henry VIII* must surely be the 1613 performance at the Globe, where some fancy special effects with a cannon resulted in the thatched roof catching fire, burning down the theatre.

❖ People have sometimes speculated that Shakespeare was a secret Roman Catholic. If so, he must have been a very secret one indeed, given that an important character *doesn't* appear in *Henry VIII*. Amid all the celebration over Elizabeth's birth, the fact that Katherine and Henry already had a daughter, who went on to become Queen Mary, persecutor of Protestants, is referred to just once.

❖ The play was originally called *All Is True*. Henry wasn't mentioned in the title until the First Folio, when the play was published as *The Famous History of the Life of King Henry the Eighth*.

## QUOTABLE LINES

'Go *with me like good angels to my end,
And, as the long divorce of steel falls on me,
Make of your prayers one sweet sacrifice,
And lift my soul to heaven.*'

'*I would not be a queen
For all the world.*'

'*Love thyself last.
Cherish those hearts that hate thee.*'

## CHAPTER FIVE
# THE TRAGEDIES

Here they are: the biggies. When people say 'Shakespeare's plays', they're usually talking about the tragedies. These contain some of the greatest, most complicated characters ever created, and are written in some of the most extraordinarily moving and beautiful language ever put to paper.

Naturally, there are some oddities. For every *Macbeth*, there's a *Titus Andronicus*; for every *Hamlet*, a *Troilus and Cressida*. Even geniuses don't knock it out of the park every time.

# ANTONY AND CLEOPATRA

Classed as a tragedy, but actually more of a historical romance, this play shows that even people over the age of 30 can fall crazily in love. Oh, and that long-distance relationships are very tricky. The play picks up shortly after *Julius Caesar* leaves off.

## PLOT

The play is set around 40 BC, and flits from Rome to Athens and Alexandria. Mark Antony is one of the three rulers (triumvirate) of the Roman Republic and he's in Egypt because it has become a territory of Rome. Falling in love with Cleopatra, Queen of Egypt, isn't in the plan, especially at his somewhat advanced age, but Antony becomes so besotted that he neglects his duties. Octavius Caesar, another member of the triumvirate, is not pleased, particularly as Antony's love-struck behaviour is the source of gossip.

Receiving news of an uprising led by a general named Pompey, along with word that his wife Fulvia has died, Antony is forced to return to Rome, though Cleopatra pleads with him to stay.

The situation in Rome gets sorted out, and Pompey signs up to a peace deal. But in order to strengthen the bond between the three members of the triumvirate, Antony is persuaded to marry Octavia, sister of Caesar. When Cleopatra finds out, she isn't a happy bunny. Antony trundles off to Athens with his new wife.

But when he discovers that Caesar has been dissing him and has gone off to do battle with Pompey, Antony decides to return to Alexandria. Now everything starts to fall apart. Back with Cleopatra, Antony decides to give all his territory to her as a present. This turns out to be a lousy decision because Caesar, having defeated Pompey, leads his army against Antony. Despite being urged not to, Antony joins up with the Egyptian Navy to fight Caesar at sea. They're defeated and retreat to Alexandria.

Antony is then defeated in another battle, when the Egyptian forces desert him. Cleopatra learns that Antony blames her for his defeat, because he thinks she betrayed him to Caesar. She angrily sends word, via a servant, that she's dead. Antony, in despair, asks his friend Eros to kill him; Eros kills himself instead. In a copycat suicide, Antony falls on his sword and is carried to Cleopatra to die in her arms. Caesar wants to take Cleopatra prisoner to be paraded through the capital but she prevents this by having poisonous snakes secretly brought to her. Dressed in her most luxurious robes, she holds an asp to her breast, is bitten and dies. Caesar gives his permission for Antony and Cleopatra to be buried together.

## IN A NUTSHELL

Antony learns the hard way that mixing business with pleasure is a bad idea.

## OTHER NOTABLE CHARACTERS

Antony's loyal general, Enobarbus, can see when Antony is making a fool of himself. When his loyalty has finally been tested to the limit, he reluctantly leaves (and later dies 'of shame' at having let Antony down). The Clown who smuggles the poisonous snakes to Cleopatra in a basket. He cracks some good jokes before Cleopatra's tragic final scene.

## BODY COUNT

Six: Antony, Cleopatra, Enobarbus, Eros; and Iras and Charmian, Cleopatra's attendants, who presumably are also bitten by a snake. Though Iras seems, puzzlingly, to die before the snakes appear, via a kiss from Cleopatra.

## DID YOU KNOW?

❖ The play is, as Andrew Dickson says, 'well-nigh unstageable', with more than 200 entrances and exits, and loads of short scenes, with people practically running across the stage by the end.

❖ Cleopatra is one of Shakespeare's most complicated and fascinating women. Not only does she have more lines than any other female character in the canon, she also gets to swan around in a magnificent gold cape.

❖ When Cleopatra says to her maid, 'let's to billiards', she's very much ahead of her time. About 1,400 years ahead, in fact, as billiards weren't invented till the fifteenth century.

❖ Before her affair with Mark Antony, which produced three children, the real-life Cleopatra was Julius Caesar's lover (they also had a child).

❖ Shakespeare relied on Plutarch's *Life of Antonius* as his key source material.

 QUOTABLE LINES

*'The triple pillar of the world transformed
Into a strumpet's fool.'*

'*The barge she sat in, like a burnished throne*
*Burned on the water. The poop was beaten gold;*
*Purple the sails, and so perfumèd that*
*The winds were love-sick with them.*
*The oars were silver,*
*Which to the tune of flutes kept stroke,*
*and made*
*The water which they beat to follow faster,*
*As amorous of their strokes.*'

'*My salad days,*
*When I was green in judgement, cold in blood.*'

'*Age cannot wither her, nor custom stale*
*Her infinite variety.*'

# CORIOLANUS

Probably dating from Shakespeare's later, Jacobean period, *Coriolanus* is one of several plays from the time that revisit the classical era (e.g. *Antony and Cleopatra* and *Pericles*). Its themes of political and military ruthlessness, and uprisings amongst the common people, have made it resonant over the intervening centuries and occasionally controversial.

## PLOT

We enter on a discontented Rome in the middle of a famine, just exploding into a revolt. Much anger is focused on Caius Martius, a successful general who may be withholding grain from the people. Martius certainly lacks the common touch and, when he tells the rioters they don't deserve grain, he adds that they should probably be executed too.

Luckily for him, Rome has other distractions in the form of an invasion by the Volscians (led by Aufidius, Martius's sworn enemy). Martius is second in command of the Roman Army under Cominius, but it's clear where the martial vigour is. His mother, Volumnia, has told her daughter-in-law that he really is something special and this proves to be more than simple maternal boasting. Despite wounds and stiff resistance, Martius conquers a Volscian city called Corioli and is given the title 'Coriolanus', meaning 'conqueror of Corioli'.

Following the path of many other successful military men, Coriolanus, pushed by his mother, decides to run for public office. While he wins the support of the Senate to become a consul, he again struggles to connect with the people. He's clearly no Eisenhower, and quickly reveals his distaste for the idea of rule by the plebs. So petulant is he that he's storming out of town almost before the Romans can banish him for his un-Republican views.

His hatred of the Roman populace overrides his lifetime of enmity with Aufidius, and Coriolanus suggests Aufidius kill him just to spite Rome, the crazy hothead. Luckily Aufidius is more interested in making use of Coriolanus's military talents, and they join forces to invade Rome. We realise though that Aufidius is a rotter and, when Coriolanus has done his dirty work, it'll be 'Goodnight, Charlie'.

In the last act we see how hell-bent on vengeance Coriolanus is. It takes a plea from his mother (accompanied by his wife and son) to talk him down. Finally, he arranges a peace treaty. Like a mafia informant, he's aware of the position this puts him in with the bad guys and, on his return to the Volscian capital, he's stabbed and trampled by an angry mob. He never could manage to be popular.

## IN A NUTSHELL

Mighty warrior is crappy politician.

## OTHER NOTABLE CHARACTERS

Brutus and Sicinius, tribunes of the people and properly sly politicos. Coriolanus doesn't stand a chance when they whip up public feeling against him.

## BODY COUNT

Though the main character is clearly extremely violent (a common production image is of Coriolanus covered in blood), the number of named characters who die is comparatively small. Cominius and Menenius (a senator) are killed in the final battle, and Coriolanus's unpopularity finally overtakes him at the end.

### DID YOU KNOW?

❖ Many scholars have suggested that *Coriolanus* was partly inspired by the Midland Revolt of 1607, a popular uprising against the enclosure of common land by the toffs. Does the play reveal where Warwickshire lad Will's sympathies lay in this conflict between peasants and the nobility? As usual with Shakespeare, you can find whatever answer you want in the text.

- ❖ Perhaps it was also inspired by Shakespeare's inside knowledge of grain-hoarding in times of famine...

- ❖ While performances of Shakespeare's plays have often been permitted during politically sensitive times, *Coriolanus* is unusual in being one of the very few to be suppressed in modern times. It was briefly banned in France in the 1930s, due to fears about fascist overtones.

## QUOTABLE LINES

*'He's a very dog to the commonalty.'*

*'You common cry of curs, whose breath I hate*
*As reek o' th' rotten fens, whose loves I prize*
*As the dead carcasses of unburied men*
*That do corrupt my air: I banish you.'*
**(A MODERN POLITICAL SPEECH-WRITER WOULD PROBABLY REPHRASE THIS A LITTLE.)**

*'Let me have war, say I. It exceeds peace as far as day does night. It's spritely walking, audible and full of vent. Peace is a very apoplexy, lethargy; mulled, deaf, sleepy, insensible; a getter of more bastard children than war's a destroyer of men.'*

*'O mother, mother!*
*What have you done? Behold, the heavens do ope,*
*The gods look down, and this unnatural scene*
*They laugh at.'*

# HAMLET

Even people who know nothing of Shakespeare have heard of *Hamlet*. It's the one with a man talking to a skull, declaiming, 'Alas, poor Yorick, I knew him well' (a misquote, incidentally). *Hamlet* is easily the most quoted piece of literature in English. There's a (probably apocryphal) story that someone read *Hamlet* and claimed not to see what the fuss was about, for it was merely a load of quotes strung together.

It contains the most famous lines of all: 'To be, or not to be, that is the question...' These words are so familiar we scarcely hear them any more; still less reflect on their astonishing power. But a good production can make you think about them properly, as though hearing them for the first time. Hamlet is an extraordinary protagonist: impulsive, indecisive, troubled, complicated, sometimes unlikeable. It's considered that his portrayal ushered in a new age of literature and, some argue, a new way of understanding human complexity.

## PLOT

Young Prince Hamlet is feeling very down. He's returned to his native Denmark from school in Germany because his father, the King, has recently died. His mother, Gertrude, has remarried in haste, to Hamlet's uncle (his father's brother), Claudius. Now Claudius is King. Hamlet suspects foul play, and this suspicion is confirmed by the appearance of his father's ghost, who tells Hamlet that Claudius murdered him by pouring poison in his ear as he slept. In order to explore the truth, Hamlet pretends to be insane, so he can say and do outrageous things he couldn't otherwise. He behaves oddly with Ophelia, though previously the two had been romantically linked, as the tabloids might put it. Ophelia's father, Polonius, a court adviser, wonders if Hamlet is maddened by love for her. But Ophelia's brother, Laertes, warns her away from Hamlet.

Hamlet, not sure whether to trust the ghost, organises a travelling troupe of actors to put on a play for the court which re-enacts the murder of his father. Claudius storms out, confirming his guilt. Hamlet berates his mother for marrying her husband's killer. Polonius is eavesdropping behind a tapestry (or 'arras') and he cries out when he hears Hamlet's accusation. Thinking it's Claudius who's hiding, Hamlet stabs into the arras, killing Polonius.

Claudius summons Hamlet's old friends, Rosencrantz and Guildenstern, and tells them to accompany him to England. The official reason is to help Hamlet recover from his madness; the truth is that Claudius has written a letter of execution for him to give to the King of England. While Hamlet is gone, Ophelia is driven mad by the murder of her father, and by Hamlet's indifference towards her, and she drowns herself.

Hamlet outwits Rosencrantz and Guildenstern, leaving them to be executed instead, and returns to Denmark. Laertes declares vengeance on him for the deaths of his father and sister, and plots with Claudius to ensure that a duel is weighted in Laertes's favour, with a poisoned blade (and a goblet of poison on standby, to make totally sure of finishing the job). But during the duel, Gertrude unwittingly drinks from the poisoned chalice and dies, and though Laertes manages to wound Hamlet with the poisoned blade, Hamlet uses it in turn to wound him back.

Laertes tells Hamlet that they're both poisoned and will very soon die. Hamlet uses the same blade to stab Claudius and makes him drink poison for good measure. The entire royal family dies, and Prince Fortinbras of Norway is left to rule Denmark – and organise all the burials.

## IN A NUTSHELL

Prince seeks vengeance and has a few existential dramas. Everyone winds up dead.

## OTHER NOTABLE CHARACTERS

Horatio, Hamlet's most trusted friend, the only main character still standing at the end of the play.

## BODY COUNT

Eight: Hamlet, Gertrude, Claudius, Ophelia, Polonius, Laertes, Rosencrantz and Guildenstern. Nine if you count Hamlet's father, killed before the action begins. Ten if you count Gonzago, the character in the play-within-a-play who enacts King Hamlet's death.

## DID YOU KNOW?

❖ *Hamlet* is Shakespeare's longest play, with 4,042 lines (or 4,024 or 4,000, depending on which source you go with) – 200 more lines than the next longest, *Coriolanus*, and more than 2,250 more lines than *The Comedy of Errors*, the shortest play. If left uncut, *Hamlet* takes around four hours to perform.

❖ It's the most filmed play (and the second most performed, after *A Midsummer Night's Dream*). Kenneth Branagh's 1996 film contains the whole text and runs to 238 minutes; critic Roger Ebert said of all the versions he'd seen, this one 'made me feel for the first time at home in that doomed royal court.'

❖ At the other end of the scale, there's Tom Stoppard's *The Fifteen Minute Hamlet*, which performs *Hamlet* in 13 minutes, followed by a two-minute version. The Reduced Shakespeare Company perform 36 of Shakespeare's plays in the first half of their show, and devote the second half to *Hamlet*, performing it several times at increasing speed. They conclude with *Hamlet* in 43 seconds (a world record), then do the play backwards at about the same speed.

❖ The 'bit with the skull' actually goes: 'Alas, poor Yorick. I knew him, Horatio.' Hamlet and Horatio are hanging out in a graveyard, speculating on who various skulls might once have belonged to. The gravedigger tells them that one skull is that of Yorick, the King's jester.

❖ Odd though the auricular poisoning seems, the death of Hamlet's father was inspired by the real-life murder of the Duke of Urbino in 1538. He was killed by a poisoned lotion which was rubbed into his ears by his barber (there's a helluva story there).

❖ The title of the play-within-the-play is *The Murder of Gonzago*, but Hamlet tells Claudius it's called *The Mousetrap*, to avoid alerting him to its content. Agatha Christie borrowed this title for her murder-mystery play, which opened in 1952 and is still going.

## QUOTABLE LINES

There are too many to list – you could practically reproduce the whole play – so I've gone with the biggies, plus some personal favourites.

*'To be, or not to be; that is the question:*
*Whether 'tis nobler in the mind to suffer*
*The slings and arrows of outrageous fortune,*
*Or to take arms against a sea of troubles,*
*And, by opposing, end them.'*

**FROM THE SAME SPEECH:**
*'To sleep, perchance to dream. Ay, there's the rub,*
*For in that sleep of death what dreams may come*
*When we have shuffled off this mortal coil*
*Must give us pause.'*

**ALSO FROM THIS SPEECH, THIS BEAUTIFUL DESCRIPTION**
**OF WHATEVER HAPPENS AFTER DEATH:**
*'But that the dread of something after death,*
*The undiscovered country from whose bourn*
*No traveller returns.'*

*'Neither a borrower nor a lender be.'*

*'Something is rotten in the state of Denmark.'*

*'This above all – to thine own self be true.'*

*'Frailty, thy name is woman.'*

*'Though this be madness,*
*yet there is method in't.'*

*'What a piece of work is a man!*
*How noble in reason, how infinite in faculty.'*

*'The lady protests too much, methinks.'*

*'The play's the thing*
*Wherein I'll catch the conscience of the King.'*

*'Brevity is the soul of wit.'*

'*Doubt thou the stars are fire,*
*Doubt that the sun doth move,*
*Doubt truth to be a liar,*
*But never doubt I love.*'

'*When sorrows come they come not single spies,*
*But in battalions.*'

# SHAKESPEARE AND ME

*Andrew Wincott is a stage and radio actor, best known as Adam on* The Archers. *He's a member of the London Shakespeare Group.*

### What was your switch-on moment?

It was a slow burn with me. Around the time of my O levels I saw a memorable production of *Much Ado About Nothing* with Judi Dench and Donald Sinden. But I really got into Shakespeare at Oxford. I had a fantastic tutor there, Peter Conrad; and I played Angelo in *Measure for Measure*. The words are written to be played. When you speak those lines they become something different altogether.

### Which is your favourite of Shakespeare's plays?

I suppose *Hamlet* has everything in it, and is so much about the theatre. Shakespeare often reaches for theatre as a metaphor. *Hamlet* is probably the greatest ever tragedy, but it traffics in comedy. It's so difficult to pin down.

**Tell us about the most memorable performance you've seen.**

Recently, Michael Sheen as Hamlet. He focused on the madness in a bold and inventive way, and Elsinore was reimagined as an asylum. Fascinating. I've seen a lot of great Hamlets. I liked Sam West's. And David Tennant's was so funny. I also really enjoyed the recent *Merchant of Venice* with Ian McDiarmid as Shylock, with Belmont depicted as Las Vegas, though I imagine it wouldn't have been everyone's cup of tea. On film, I love Orson Welles's *Chimes at Midnight*, which puts several of the Henry plays together to brilliant effect. Welles's Shakespeare films were very influential for me; I love his *Othello*, which was filmed in Morocco.

**Which Shakespeare character have you most enjoyed playing?**

I loved playing Jaques in *As You Like It* (partly because of the 'All the world's a stage' speech), Malvolio in *Twelfth Night* (whom I played like Kenneth Williams) and Mercutio in *Romeo and Juliet*. Mercutio has probably the greatest death. No one wants him to die as he's such fun. He's punning even as he dies: 'Ask for me tomorrow, and you shall find me a grave man.'

> **How would you persuade somebody to give Shakespeare a chance?**
>
> If you listen to the language, it will give you the emotions. The rhythm tells you how to feel and breathe it. Iambic pentameter is the rhythm of the human heart. And of course, both Shakespeare and *The Archers* are rooted in the heart of England!

# JULIUS CAESAR

*Julius Caesar* is a short sharp shock of a play, scarcely longer than a piece of frippery such as *The Merry Wives of Windsor*. Nonetheless, it is epic in scale, with great themes of betrayal and class struggle woven through it, as well as a slew of quotable lines and marvellous speeches. The play has often been used over the centuries as a commentary on current political affairs, but it's a terrific piece of theatre outside of that, boasting one of the main features of Shakespeare's genius: complex and conflicted characters.

## PLOT

We enter on triumphant Julius Caesar returning to Rome from victory in a civil war. While the hoi polloi are dancing, not everyone is thrilled by the war's outcome. Also, some suspect Caesar is flirting with kingship (bad news in a republic) and generally getting too big for his boots. So cocky is he that he even dismisses dire portents uttered by a soothsayer ('Beware the ides of March'), and you know trouble can't be far behind.

It's closer than Caesar thinks, as members of his entourage, Cassius and Brutus, hatch a plot to kill him. Despite being the title character, Caesar is despatched in pretty short order (at the beginning of Act 3). It's a famous scene, in which he's stabbed in the back literally and metaphorically by his close colleagues, with Brutus last. The power of this scene is closely rivalled by Brutus's subsequent funeral oration, where he clarifies that the whole deal was for the good of Rome ('not that I loved Caesar less, but that I loved Rome more'). This wins over the crowd but is topped by the speech of Caesar's close friend Mark Antony ('Friends, Romans, countrymen...'), which proclaims Caesar as a noble fellow, and adds in some monetary incentives for the fickle mob.

Brutus and Cassius rapidly find themselves in hot water and, this being the classical world, that means war. Antony joins forces with Octavius (Caesar's adopted son and heir), and we're soon in full battle mode. Brutus endures a very bad, guilt-ridden night on the eve of the most important battle. He's already coping with the death of his wife, and then he's visited by Caesar's ghost. The battle doesn't go well for him and Cassius, and they take the gentleman's way out, Brutus via suicide and Cassius by getting his servant Pindarus to kill him. Brutus is given a noble burial and some complimentary words from Antony. Octavius Caesar and Antony take over; all is then set for Shakespeare's next Roman blockbuster, *Antony and Cleopatra*.

## IN A NUTSHELL

Julius Caesar is killed by his friend for the good of the Roman Republic. Friend feels terrible about it and the Republic is pretty much doomed anyway.

## OTHER NOTABLE CHARACTERS

Casca, one of the conspirators, first to stab Caesar during the assassination. Portia, Brutus's much-loved wife, who's used to Brutus telling her all his problems, and gets distressed when he becomes guilt-ridden and distant.

## BODY COUNT

Six. Four by stabbing: Caesar, Brutus, Cassius (was that really in Pindarus's job description?) and Titinius, Cassius's friend, who kills himself when he sees Cassius dead. Portia kills herself by swallowing hot coals (ugh!). Plus there's pretty much the most unfortunate death in the entire canon: Cinna the poet is innocently walking along the street when he's mistaken for Cinna the conspirator and is torn to pieces by a mob.

### DID YOU KNOW?

❖ Abraham Lincoln's assassin, John Wilkes Booth, appeared in a production of *Julius Caesar* five months before Lincoln's death, though he played Antony rather than Brutus.

❖ The real-life Caesar was stabbed 23 times, but only one of the wounds was fatal.

## QUOTABLE LINES

'The fault, dear Brutus, is not in our stars,
But in ourselves.'

'Cowards die many times before their deaths;
The valiant never taste of death but once.'

'Yon Cassius has a lean and hungry look.'

'Et tu, Bruté? – Then fall, Caesar.'

'But I am constant as the Northern Star.'

'Cry, "havoc!" and let slip the dogs of war.'

'There is a tide in the affairs of men.'

'Friends, Romans, countrymen,
lend me your ears.
I come to bury Caesar, not to praise him.'

'This was the most unkindest cut of all.'

'This was the noblest Roman of them all.'

'And say to all the world "This was a man".'

# KING LEAR

Those who love *King Lear* really love it, considering it the greatest of Shakespeare's plays; others find it unremittingly bleak and cruel. It's not completely surprising that until the nineteenth century a version with a happy ending, adapted by Irish poet Nahum Tate, was usually performed instead.

## PLOT

King Lear, an elderly ruler in ancient Britain, realises it's time to take things a bit easier, so he decides to divide up his kingdom between his three daughters and spend his remaining years staying with each of them in turn as their guest. He asks them to tell him how much they love him. Goneril and Regan, both ambitious, go completely over the top, exaggerating their affection, hoping to secure a bigger share of the kingdom. Cordelia, his favourite, tells him simply and truthfully that she loves him as a daughter should, no more, no less. The King is so angry that she hasn't flattered him that he divides the kingdom in two, giving half each to Regan and Goneril and nothing to Cordelia. She's quickly married off to the King of France, with no dowry, and leaves the country.

Things now start to go wrong. When the King stays with Goneril, he finds she doesn't treat him with enough respect. He throws a tantrum and heads off to stay with Regan, only to find she treats him even worse! In a fury, he decides he'd rather fend for himself than tolerate such disrespect, so, during a thunderstorm, he leaves Regan's castle with the loyal Earl of Kent for company. Living rough, he learns how hard life can be for ordinary people and eventually goes mad.

When Goneril, Regan and her husband, the Duke of Cornwall, hear that a French Army has landed at Dover and that Lear is on his way there to find Cordelia, they arrest and torture the Duke of Gloucester, who has helped him. The King is reunited with Cordelia and his sanity is restored, but the French Army is defeated, and Lear and Cordelia are imprisoned.

Alongside the main story, there are two brothers, the sons of the Duke of Gloucester. Edmond resents the fact that he's the illegitimate and Edgar the legitimate son. He tricks his father into thinking that Edgar is plotting to kill him, and Edgar has to go into hiding, disguising himself as a mad beggar. The ambitious Edmond gains power by becoming the lover of both Goneril and Regan. Edgar returns and kills Edmond, who admits just before he dies that he has ordered the execution of the King and Cordelia. This confession comes too late to save Cordelia, and King Lear dies of grief with his arms around his dead daughter. Finally, he comes to see that Cordelia spoke the truth when she said she loved him, and that her sisters were dishonest and just saying what he wanted to hear.

## IN A NUTSHELL

A king is taken in by flattery, makes a bad decision, goes mad, dies.

## OTHER NOTABLE CHARACTERS

The Fool, who uses jokes and riddles to show the King when he's being an idiot.

## BODY COUNT

This is in the *Titus Andronicus* ballpark – something between nine and eleven deaths, depending on how you count them.

Really, just about everyone cops it: King Lear (grief); Cordelia (hanged); Regan (poisoned by Goneril); Goneril (suicide); the Duke of Gloucester (heart failure after torture); Edmond, Oswald, the Duke of Cornwall and his servant (all stabbed). The Fool disappears – most interpretations assume he has been killed. Finally, Kent, a nobleman and friend of Lear, hints at the end of the play that he'll kill himself so as to follow Lear.

## DID YOU KNOW?

- ❖ Even George Bernard 'Not Keen on Shakespeare' Shaw said, 'No man will ever write a better tragedy than *Lear*.'

- ❖ Jonathan Pryce, who played Lear in 2012, said, 'Tradition dictates that you should play Lear while you're young enough to lift Cordelia up and carry her. I was sixty-five, and I put my back out doing it – I couldn't carry her for the entire second half of the production's run.'

- ❖ Ian McKellen, who played Lear in 1997, appeared naked during Lear's madness. Germaine Greer's review said: 'for many of us the only memorable moment in Trevor Nunn's latest production of *King Lear* is when Ian McKellen drops his trousers and displays his impressive genitalia to the audience.'

- ❖ The most notable adaptation is the award-winning *Ran* (which means 'chaos') directed by Akira Kurosawa, at the time the most expensive Japanese film ever made.

## QUOTABLE LINES

*'When we are born, we cry that we are come*
*To this great stage of fools.'*

*'Nothing will come of nothing.'*

*'How sharper than a serpent's tooth it is*
*To have a thankless child.'*

*'I am a man more sinned against than sinning.'*

*'As flies to wanton boys are we to th' gods;*
*They kill us for their sport.'*

*'Thou art a soul in bliss, but I am bound*
*Upon a wheel of fire, that mine own tears*
*Do scald like molten lead.'*

*'Why should a dog, a horse, a rat have life,*
*And thou no breath at all?'*
**(LEAR, MOURNING OVER THE BODY OF CORDELIA.)**

*'We that are young*
*Shall never see so much, nor live so long.'*

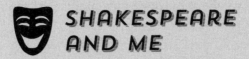

# SHAKESPEARE AND ME

*David Bellwood is Senior Marketing and Access Officer at Shakespeare's Globe. He has worked there for ten seasons.*

## What was your switch-on moment?

Reading Lamb's *Tales from Shakespeare* as a child. I still have my school project that I wrote after reading them, aged ten. Something in the stories really captured my imagination, but I think the fact that all the adult world seemed to know these stories was really attractive to me.

## Which is your favourite of Shakespeare's plays?

Favourites are difficult. I find that as life changes so do my reactions to the various voices in Shakespeare's plays. At the moment I would probably say *Hamlet* or *As You Like It*, but I recently returned to *King Lear* and it resonates with me really beautifully at the moment. One of the most important elements to Shakespeare's success and longevity is his ability to capture the varying ages and dilemmas of life, so I am always a little bit suspicious when people say they have one absolute favourite play.

**Tell us about the most memorable performance you've seen.**

Probably the last performance of *Henry IV, Part I* at the Globe. The run had been extended and the atmosphere was surreal. No one wanted that production to come to an end.

**Which Shakespeare character would you most like to meet?**

Titania. She's immortal and keeps interesting friends. If I couldn't meet her, I wouldn't mind spending a weekend with Beatrice and Benedick.

**How would you persuade somebody to give Shakespeare a chance?**

My role at the Globe involves helping deaf and disabled people access our work. I often have to discuss the plays with people of varying neurodiversity and with varying senses. A blind patron, for example, might focus heavily on those passages of a play that describe the environment of the scene much more closely than a person whose vision is not impaired. The work really opens up the plays in new and exciting ways for me, and I hope my work helps invite increasing numbers of people to engage with Shakespeare's writing.

So I'd say, go to the Globe! With tickets only £5, they're cheaper than a pint. Alternatively, try watching a film adaptation – there are some excellent examples out there, such as Joss Whedon's *Much Ado About Nothing*.

# MACBETH

*Macbeth* (ssh, I mean 'the Scottish play') is Shakespeare's shortest tragedy, packed full of violence, psychological tension, memorable lines and one of the most fascinating marriages ever put on paper. It's a classic Caledonian caper of carnage, a tale of what can go wrong when you heed the advice of portents and an overly ambitious spouse – Lady Macbeth, one of the great Shakespearean archetypes, ambitious, terrifying and brave.

## PLOT

Fresh from military success, Macbeth and his fellow general Banquo stumble across three witches who tell Macbeth he's on the fast track for promotion: from Thane of Glamis (which he is already) to Thane of Cawdor, and pretty soon King. Almost immediately, Macbeth learns that he's now Thane of Cawdor, the previous Thane having been sentenced to death.

Back at the castle, Macbeth confides in his wife, the super-ambitious Lady Macbeth. While he wobbles, she convinces him to 'screw your courage to the sticking-place' and bump off their guest for the evening, King Duncan of Scotland. To cover his tracks, Macbeth kills Duncan's guards when he 'discovers' the dead Duncan the next morning. He immediately assumes the mantle of top dog.

Concerned about the witches' other prophecy, that Banquo will be greater than him, the new King sends assassins to kill him. Banquo cops it, but his son, Fleance, flees to England. At a feast for his investiture, Macbeth is tormented by the appearance of Banquo's bloody ghost, who chooses to sit on the throne, sending the monarch mad.

Lady M. tries to calm her husband down, but the superstitious King heads off to see the three witches again. They tell him to beware of Macduff, a nobleman who's against Macbeth's kingship, but that Macbeth can't be harmed by any man born of woman. They add that he'll be safe until Birnam Wood comes to Dunsinane Castle. Macbeth interprets all this to mean he'll be OK – how can a wood come to his castle, for starters? Having begun on a crazed killing spree, he continues, sending his henchmen to see off the Macduffs. They get his wife, children and court, but not the man himself, who flees to England to join Duncan's son, Malcolm.

Meantime, Lady Macbeth sees the writing on the wall, goes properly potty and kills herself. Duncan's son Malcolm, a peeved Macduff, and a ragtag and bobtail of Englishers cut down Birnam Wood and use the branches to disguise how few troops they have as they march towards Chez Macbeth.

*Hang on, isn't this a forest marching towards my castle?* our anti-hero ponders anxiously. Then he relaxes, remembering the 'born of woman' prediction. But Macbeth should have checked the local maternity records. Macduff was 'from his mother's womb untimely ripp'd' – born by C-section, in other words. Macduff cuts off Macbeth's head, and Malcolm takes the crown of Scotland.

## IN A NUTSHELL

*McGame of Thrones* meets *The Apprentice*, with knives. It's really the story of a dysfunctional marriage, a *folie à deux*, which ends in a bloodbath.

## OTHER NOTABLE CHARACTERS

Hecate, ruler of the witches; and the Porter, who provides some much-needed comic relief.

## BODY COUNT

Ten principals. Though one of the bloodiest plays, many of the deaths take place off stage, including King Duncan, Lady Macbeth and Macbeth himself. Other deaths include Duncan's two guards; Banquo; Macduff's wife, children and entire staff; and Young Siward, son of the general of the English army.

## DID YOU KNOW?

❖ Macbeth is a real figure from history. Shakespeare based the play on accounts of the Scottish Kings in *Holinshed's Chronicles*, a book of British history, though the actual events were rather different to the play. *Macbeth* is also believed to have taken some inspiration from the Gunpowder Plot in 1605.

❖ It's likely that *Macbeth* was written as a way of honouring the new Scottish King of England, James I, who took the throne in 1603. Banquo was one of his ancestors.

❖ In Shakespeare's day, when people genuinely believed in the power of witches, the weird sisters would have had the power to absolutely terrorise an audience. King James I was an authority on witches, having written a book about them, *Daemonologie*.

❖ The play has the reputation of being cursed, and in the theatre is always referred to superstitiously as 'the Scottish play' rather than by its title. If you accidentally name it, you have to perform certain rituals, including spitting and turning round.

❖ Polanski's violent 1971 film version, starring Francesca Annis as Lady M., also featured, unbelievably, Keith Chegwin as Fleance.

❖ Akira Kurosawa's 1957 film *Throne of Blood* is a much-admired retelling of the story, which uses styles from Noh and kabuki theatre. Andrew Dickson calls it 'the most perfect Shakespearean movie in existence'.

❖ Macbeth's cry of 'Lay on, Macduff' (meaning 'Let's get this fight started') has forever been misquoted as 'Lead on, Macduff'. Though the latter is a rather useful phrase for getting small children moving on a walk.

 QUOTABLE LINES

Practically the whole of *Macbeth* could be in this section; it's one of the most quotable plays. Every schoolchild knows 'out, damned spot', even if they think it refers to a particularly stubborn blackhead. Most of the best lines are shared amongst Macbeth, Lady Macbeth and the three witches.

**MACBETH:**

*'If it were done when 'tis done, then 'twere well
It were done quickly.'*

*'Is this a dagger which I see before me,
The handle toward my hand?
Come, let me clutch thee.
I have thee not, and yet I see thee still.'*

*'This is a sorry sight.'*

*'Tomorrow, and tomorrow, and tomorrow
Creeps in this petty pace from day to day.'*

*'Out, out, brief candle.
Life's but a walking shadow, a poor player
That struts and frets his hour upon the stage,
And then is heard no more. It is a tale
Told by an idiot, full of sound and fury,
Signifying nothing.'*

**LADY MACBETH:**

*'Come, you spirits
That tend on mortal thoughts, unsex me here.'*

*'Out, damned spot; out, I say!'*

*'Yet who would have thought the old man to
have had so much blood in him?'*

'What's done is done.'

'All the perfumes of Arabia will not
sweeten this little hand.'

**THE WITCHES:**
'When shall we three meet again?
In thunder, lightning, or in rain?'

'Double, double, toil and trouble,
Fire burn, and cauldron bubble.'

'Fair is foul, and foul is fair.'

'By the pricking of my thumbs,
Something wicked this way comes.'

**MACDUFF GETS A COUPLE:**
'One fell swoop.'

'Macduff was from his mother's womb
Untimely ripped.'

**AND MALCOLM GETS ONE:**
'Nothing in his life
Became him like the leaving it.'

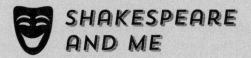

## SHAKESPEARE AND ME

*Polly Brown is a sales assistant at the RSC Theatre gift shop in Stratford-upon-Avon. She has an MA in Shakespeare Studies.*

### What was your switch-on moment?

It was when I was 14 and studying *Macbeth*. I was caught up by the darkness, the sense of nature imploding. The language seemed different from other Shakespeare plays – more choppy and ominous.

### Tell us about the most memorable performance you've seen.

It wasn't actually at the RSC! It was *Othello* at the National, around 2013. It wasn't afraid to get down and dirty. For instance, Othello's epileptic fit took place in a toilet stall.

### Which Shakespeare character would you most like to meet?

Coriolanus. I'm absolutely fascinated by a guy who's so atrociously cold and vicious. I'd also like to meet Volumnia, his mother.

# OTHELLO

Like *The Merchant of Venice*, *Othello* is set in the city of palaces and canals; this setting provides a place where people from wildly different backgrounds can meet. Most likely written in the early 1600s, the play deals with complex themes: race, social acceptance, trust and especially jealousy. It also contains one of Shakespeare's most famous and villainous villains: Iago.

## PLOT

Othello is a commander of Venetian military forces. He's 'Moorish' (black), and has eloped with Desdemona, the (white) daughter of a Venetian senator. While this is initially accepted, other than by Desdemona's dad, we can see that this might not end well.

Othello is in action in Cyprus, with Desdemona along for the ride. Also present are Cassio, his lieutenant, and Iago, a lowly ensign (junior officer). Iago resents Cassio, who's been promoted above him, and Othello, for doing the promoting. Iago's machinations lead Cassio into a brawl with Roderigo, a Venetian who's in love with Desdemona, and Cassio is soon out of favour with Othello. The scheming is only just starting, however; after Iago gets Desdemona to intercede on Cassio's behalf, he begins to suggest to Othello that she may not be entirely faithful.

Iago sneaks Desdemona's handkerchief into Cassio's room. When Othello sees that Bianca, Cassio's mistress, has the hankie, he becomes convinced that Desdemona and Cassio are lovers. Othello is soon accusing Desdemona of all sorts. Under Iago's influence, he knocks her about and plans to kill her, and things become well out of hand. Roderigo is manipulated by Iago into attacking Cassio, but Iago wounds Cassio himself and kills Roderigo. Othello smothers Desdemona and, too late, Iago's villainy is revealed. Othello, after a botched attempt to kill Iago, then kills himself.

## IN A NUTSHELL

Black military commander with a few trust and impulse control issues thinks he can marry into the higher reaches of white Venetian society. He is wrong.

## OTHER NOTABLE CHARACTERS

Emilia, Desdemona's faithful servant and Iago's wife. She's the means by which Iago gets the crucial hankie, and is central in convincing Othello, though too late, of his wife's innocence. Just quite what she's doing with Iago in the first place is something of a mystery, as she's shown to be considerably wiser than her mistress in the world of men.

## BODY COUNT

The last act has the bodies piling up in a way that can only be described as Shakespearean. Desdemona, Roderigo and Emilia are all murdered. Othello commits suicide. Cassio is only wounded, as is Iago, though he's sentenced to execution at the end.

## DID YOU KNOW?

❖ Othello has the third largest number of speeches in all the plays, only pipped by Hamlet and Richard III. But if you count the roles by lines rather than speeches, Iago is the clear winner in this play, with 200 more lines than Othello.

❖ Iago is one of Shakespeare's greatest villains, and yet his motives remain foggy. Repressed homosexuality, envy, addiction to power, psychopathic tendencies – all these have been proposed as possible reasons for his actions.

❖ Awkwardly to modern eyes, Othello has often been played by white actors, with Olivier, Stanislavsky and Orson Welles, amongst many others, blacking up. Welles's film version is worth seeing nonetheless for the famous Roderigo-Cassio fight set in a Turkish bath (borne of necessity, as the actors' costumes hadn't arrived).

### QUOTABLE LINES

*'I will wear my heart upon my sleeve.'*

*'O, beware, my lord, of jealousy.*
*It is the green-eyed monster which doth mock*
*The meat it feeds on.'*

*'Tis neither here nor there.'*

*'I kissed thee ere I killed thee.*
*No way but this:*
*Killing myself, to die upon a kiss.'*

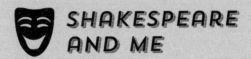

## SHAKESPEARE AND ME

*Georgianna Ziegler, Head of Reference at the Folger Shakespeare Library in Washington, D.C., has curated several Shakespeare exhibitions, including America's Shakespeare as part of the commemoration of the 400th anniversary of his death.*

**Tell us about the most memorable performance you've seen.**

Antony Sher as Richard III for the RSC in 1984. I also like the Baz Luhrmann *Romeo + Juliet* film, and thought the recent National Theatre *Othello* with Adrian Lester was the best production I've ever seen of that play.

**Which Shakespeare character would you most like to meet?**

Probably Rosalind from *As You Like It.*

**How would you persuade somebody to give Shakespeare a chance?**

I'd send them off to see a really good production, such as the NT *Othello* mentioned above, or Branagh's *Henry V*, then ask them how they see it relating to the lives and concerns of themselves and people they know.

# ROMEO AND JULIET

*Romeo and Juliet* was one of the first plays ever to feature romantic love as a central story, and perhaps the first to feature an on-stage kiss. Enduringly, endlessly popular, it's up there with *Hamlet* and *A Midsummer Night's Dream* as one of Shakespeare's most-performed works. Although classed as a tragedy, it has plenty of comedy, and a bit of everything else to boot: great fights, terrific love scenes, cracking roles and the ultimate teenage defy-the-parents storyline.

## PLOT

We're in Verona, Italy, where the young Juliet Capulet falls for the dishy Romeo Montague. But their families have a long-standing feud (we never find out why), so the lovers have to meet in secret. The most famous of these meetings is when Romeo calls up to Juliet as she stands on her balcony. Ah, romance!

With the help of the handy Friar Laurence, they secretly get married. Things immediately take a nasty turn, however, as a fight breaks out amongst the local hothead lads. They bite their thumbs at each other (an old insult, rather like flipping the middle finger) and Tybalt, Juliet's cousin, challenges Romeo to a duel. Romeo refuses because he's secretly related to Tybalt now. Romeo's wingman, Mercutio, takes the challenge instead but is killed. In a rage, Romeo kills Tybalt, and is banished from Verona.

Juliet's family unsurprisingly now hates the Montagues more than ever, but Juliet forgives her man. Her mother, not realising Juliet is already married, starts agitating for her to wed the unappealing Count Paris. To avoid this fate, Juliet turns to the Friar for help. He suggests she take a weird potion that will make her appear to be dead for two days. (Where can I get one of those?) The message to explain all this to the banished Romeo never reaches him, alas, and on finding Juliet apparently dead in the family crypt, Romeo takes poison. Juliet awakes, finds him dead by her side, seizes his dagger and kills herself. When the two families turn up to find this horrible scene, they realise what their bickering has caused, and sadly resolve to end their feud. Better late than never, chaps.

## IN A NUTSHELL

Boy meets girl, their families don't approve, they kill themselves.

## OTHER NOTABLE CHARACTERS

Juliet's nurse, who is good comic relief.

## BODY COUNT

Six: Romeo and Juliet (both on stage, dead, at the end); Mercutio; Tybalt; Lady Montague (dies off stage, of grief at Romeo's exile); and Count Paris (stabbed by Romeo in a fight).

## DID YOU KNOW?

- ❖ When Juliet toddles on to her balcony and cries, 'O Romeo, Romeo, wherefore art thou Romeo?' she doesn't mean, 'Oy, lad, show yourself!' 'Wherefore' means 'why'. So she's saying, 'Why do you have to be Romeo (i.e. from the Montague family)?' Nonetheless, a great many Juliets have made, and doubtless will continue to make, the universal gesture of searching with a hand shading their eyes.

- ❖ The play is based on a 1562 poem by Arthur Brooke called *The Tragicall Historye of Romeus and Juliet*.

- ❖ Juliet is 13 when she meets Romeo, but we aren't told how old he is. Various speculative accounts place him at anything from 15 to his early twenties, but he's usually portrayed as being just a little older than Juliet, around 16 or 17.

- ❖ The first time Romeo and Juliet meet, their dialogue (which begins with Romeo holding her hand and saying, 'If I profane with my unworthiest hand…') is in the form of a sonnet.

❖ Verona was considered a classy place in Elizabethan times. These days it styles itself as the 'city of love', with 'Juliet's tomb' and 'Juliet's balcony' as stops on the tourist trail. You can even write to 'Juliet' in Verona and ask for her advice about your own love life (and get a reply!).

❖ Zefferelli, who directed a popular film version in 1968 starring seventeen-year-old Olivia Hussey, apparently wanted Paul McCartney for Romeo. (In the end the part was played by a little-known actor called Leonard Whiting.)

❖ There are countless adaptations, including Peter Ustinov's satire *Romanoff and Juliet*; *Bollywood Queen*, about the forbidden romance between a Gujarati girl and a Scottish boy (played by James McAvoy); *Warm Bodies*, a zombie version; *Romeo x Juliet*, a Japanese anime TV series; and the animated *Gnomeo & Juliet*, in which a gnome belonging to Mrs Montague becomes enamoured of a gnome in the garden of Mr Capulet. That one, at least, has a happy ending.

❖ The phrase 'wild goose chase' first appears in *Romeo and Juliet*, though ascertaining whether Shakespeare invented it or was merely the first to get it in print has proved – yes! – to be something of a wild goose chase.

## QUOTABLE LINES

*'But soft, what light through
yonder window breaks?'*

*'What's in a name?
That which we call a rose
By any other name would smell as sweet.'*

*'Parting is such sweet sorrow.'*

*'A plague o' both your houses.'*

*'A pair of star-crossed lovers take their life.'*

*'Love is a smoke made with the fume of sighs.'*

*'For never was a story of more woe
Than this of Juliet and her Romeo.'*

## SHAKESPEARE AND ME

*Grace Upcraft has worked as a dresser in the
costume department at Chichester Festival Theatre.
Plays she has dressed for include* Antony and
Cleopatra *and* Kiss Me, Kate.

### What was your switch-on moment?

This came when I was about 14 years old and about to start studying *Macbeth* at school. My parents took me to see an open-air performance of it to inspire me. At 14, I must admit, *Macbeth* wasn't my favourite. However, the following week we also saw *Twelfth Night* by the same company and I found it very funny. It sparked an interest to learn more of his work.

### Tell us about the most memorable performance you've seen.

It was a production of *Romeo and Juliet* at the Theatre Royal in Winchester, where I was studying creative writing. I always enjoy the costumes and set pieces of Shakespeare plays but this particular performance was a modern-day adaptation. The characters wore present-day clothing and the sets were also present day. Yet the script was untouched and this made for an intriguing performance. Instead of being distracted by the beautiful costumes and sets, I instead paid more attention to the words that they were saying.

### How would you persuade somebody to give Shakespeare a chance?

Shakespeare is such a huge part of the arts and literary world and will continue to be so. It has been adapted in so many ways for everyone to enjoy

For example, the film *10 Things I Hate About You* and the musical *Kiss Me, Kate* were both adapted from *The Taming of the Shrew*. Everyone should give Shakespeare a chance because his work will always have an influence over what we learn in school, what we see at the theatre and things we may read, as writers continue to be influenced by him.

# TIMON OF ATHENS

This odd little morality piece, another of the problem plays, is believed to be a collaboration with playwright Thomas Middleton. It concerns a rich man who becomes disillusioned by humanity, and the themes of greed and cynicism about wealth perhaps speak to us more forcibly now than they did in Shakespeare's own time.

## PLOT

Timon, a nobleman in ancient Athens, is well liked as a generous man. Too generous, actually, for he's soon bankrupt, and finds that the flattering friends who were happy to eat his food aren't so friendly when it comes to a loan. Furious, Timon invites them to one last banquet but serves only stones in warm water. Way to make a point, Timon. He blasts off a diatribe about false friends and the world in general, and chucks some water at them for an encore. He then storms off into the wilderness to reside in a cave, living off roots and, presumably, his righteous indignation.

Meanwhile, a soldier called Alcibiades has gone in to bat for one of his men who's been sentenced to death by the Senate. Being a thorn in the Senate's side, Alcibiades gets himself banished, and plans revenge against Athens. He links up with Timon, who, in a lucky yet ironic move, has dug up a load of gold while foraging for food. Timon gives some gold to Alcibiades in exchange for him destroying Athens. Timon also gives gold to three thieves, so that they too will make a mess of Athens, but they decide to go straight instead. Even more misanthropically, Timon pays some prostitutes to spread sexually transmitted diseases amongst the populace.

The senators negotiate with Alcibiades at the city gates. He agrees to spare Athens and only punish the people who insulted his best mate Timon or himself. Timon's former friends ask Timon for help, but he bitterly offers them the tree outside his cave – to hang themselves on. When the enemies are handed over, Alcibiades agrees to make peace. But it's too late for Timon to get any joy from this, for word comes that he has died, alone in his cave.

## IN A NUTSHELL

Generous chap has a complete personality shift and becomes a people-hating recluse.

## OTHER NOTABLE CHARACTERS

Flavius, Timon's steward, who tries in vain to tell his heedless boss that he's running out of money. Timon eventually realises his servant is the most loyal of his friends. Apemantus, a philosopher who's sceptical about Timon's motives, thinking he was trying to buy friendship in the first place.

## BODY COUNT

Just Timon; if his frenemies are to be punished by death, that happens after the play abruptly ends.

---

### DID YOU KNOW?

❖ Theories abound about the writing of this play, in particular its unsatisfyingly un-Shakespearean ending. That might simply be because it was written with someone else. But there's speculation that it's an unfinished play and Shakespeare died before completing it; or he was depressed and broke down while writing it. Lots of theories, as always.

❖ Unusually for a Shakespeare play, the main character has no family or spouse.

❖ Thomas Middleton was no minor collaborator; he went on to write many popular plays and was considered one of the greatest playwrights of the age (T. S. Eliot thought him surpassed only by Shakespeare).

❖ Nicholas Hytner's 2012 production for the National Theatre was set in present-day London in the midst of the financial and banking crisis. The play came into its own as a sharp commentary on the nature of wealth and corruption.

---

## QUOTABLE LINES

*''Tis not enough to help the feeble up,
But to support him after.'*
(TIMON IS JUST TOO NICE! AT
THE START, ANYWAY.)

*'Men shut their doors against a setting sun.'*

*'We have seen better days.'*

*'The moon's an arrant thief,
And her pale fire she snatches from the sun.'*

# TITUS ANDRONICUS

Famous for being the most bloodily violent of Shakespeare's plays, *Titus* is thought to be an early composition, perhaps the first tragedy he wrote – which might explain all the tomato ketchup. It's certainly stronger on the inventiveness of the deaths than on the psychology. It's all about vengeance, this play. Vengeance, and pies.

## PLOT

The Roman Emperor has died, and Marcus Andronicus declares the successor will be his brother, Titus. But Titus, having just returned from fighting the Goths for ten years, is battle-weary and doesn't want to be emperor. He votes instead for Saturninus, who is duly elected. Titus is rather busy anyway, first burying the many sons he lost in battle, and then jangling the nerves of his prisoners,

Tamora, Queen of the Goths, and her sons. In fact, he murders her eldest son, just to show who's boss (it's a sacrificial rite, apparently).

Saturninus asks if he can marry Titus's daughter Lavinia, and Titus agrees; but Lavinia was already promised to Saturninus's brother, Bassianus. Arguing about this with his family, Titus kills his son Mutius. He really ought to have put that sword down before he got in a mood as he's fast running out of sons. Saturninus marries Tamora instead, though she carries on seeing her lover, Aaron. Bassianus finds out about this affair, so Tamora has two of her sons, Chiron and Demetrius, kill him. She and Aaron then frame two of Titus's sons for the murder. Next, Aaron encourages the easily led Chiron and Demetrius to rape Lavinia; afterwards they cut off her hands and tongue. *For God's sake, people.* The hand-cutting starts a copycat trend, for Aaron tells Titus that Saturninus will spare his sons if he's sent Titus's hand. Titus takes the hit (or cut), but Aaron lied; in return for his hand, Titus receives the heads of his two sons.

Now, having seen the mutilated Lavinia, Titus is *really* mad. He sends his last remaining son, Lucius, to join the army of their former enemy the Goths, and make an attack on Rome. You'd think this would be certain doom for Lucius, but in fact he's just about the only person to make it to the end of the play in one piece.

In the midst of this, Tamora gives birth to Aaron's baby, but she wants it killed because the baby has inherited Aaron's dark skin and anyway, what's another killing? Aaron rescues the baby but as there's a moment with no one being killed, he murders the baby's nurse (the official reason is to keep her quiet).

Titus seems to lose his mind, understandably. Tamora takes advantage of his apparent weakness, but Titus is only pretending. He tricks her, kills Chiron and Demetrius and – in the number-one most bizarre Shakespearean death – has them baked into a pie which Tamora unwittingly eats. Titus then kills his daughter Lavinia (*what?!* To save her shame, allegedly), and it all goes completely Tarantino crazy, blood everywhere. Titus, Tamora and Saturninus all cop it. Somehow Aaron makes it out, but not for long, because Lucius returns and buries him alive, throwing Tamora's body to the beasts for good measure. And that is how Lucius gets to be the new emperor of Rome. (I think I'll go for a quiet lie-down after all that.)

## IN A NUTSHELL

The enmity between Titus Andronicus and Queen Tamora destroys everyone in the vicinity, in a great frothing bloodbath.

## OTHER NOTABLE CHARACTERS

Martius and Quintus, the beheaded sons of Titus.

## BODY COUNT

Nine deaths take place on stage, but there are a staggering 14 in total: Titus; Tamora; Aaron; Saturninus; Bassianus; Lavinia; Chiron, Demetrius and Alarbus (Tamora's sons); Martius, Quintus and Mutius (Titus's sons); the nurse; and a random clown who's hanged. That's not including all Titus's other sons who died in battle before the story started. There's also the death of a 'black ill-favoured fly' – the only death that seems to make an impression on the traumatised Titus. (This is made much of in Spymonkey's play *The Complete Deaths* (2016), which wittily recreates all the on-stage deaths in Shakespeare's plays.)

## DID YOU KNOW?

❖ One of the stage directions reads, '*Enter a Messenger, with two heads and a hand*'. You'd hope the young Shakespeare might have paused a bit at that.

❖ Some think *Titus* was written in collaboration with the playwright George Peele, possibly to pass the blame for this lesser play on to someone else. Others, such as Harold Bloom, believe *Titus Andronicus* was written as a parody, so ridiculously exaggerated is the violence.

❖ At the 2003 RSC production, the National Blood Service parked their van outside, hoping for blood donations from theatregoers (hilarious, guys!). In a production at the Globe in 2014, a sizeable number of the audience fainted, including the theatre reviewer of the *Independent*, who therefore missed an act. She described it as 'exceptional', if 'almost unwatchable'.

❖ It's been calculated that there are 5.2 atrocities per act, in a five-act play. More than one commentator (Jonathan Bate and Charles Spencer to name two) have described it as an Elizabethan slasher movie.

❖ Though Titus is a fictional character, some of the historical facts and settings of the play are real. For instance, between 300 and 500 AD, the Goths from Germany and nearby territories did attempt to threaten the supremacy of the Roman Empire.

## QUOTABLE LINES

*'These words are razors to my wounded heart.'*

*'Vengeance is in my heart, death in my hand,*
*Blood and revenge are hammering in my head.'*
**(FEELINGS ARE RUNNING HIGH, CLEARLY.)**

*'How if that fly had a father, brother?*
*How would he hang his slender gilded wings*
*And buzz lamenting dirges in the air!*
*Poor harmless fly,*
*That with his pretty buzzing melody*
*Came here to make us merry – and thou*
*hast killed him.'*
**(TITUS FAILS TO KEEP A**
**SANE PERSPECTIVE.)**

*'I have not another tear to shed.'*
**(I'M NOT SURPRISED!)**

# TROILUS AND CRESSIDA

There's no getting away from it: *Troilus and Cressida* is a strange play, impossible to pigeonhole. In the First Folio it's not listed in the table of contents, probably because it was added rather late, squeezed in between the histories and the tragedies, as if in afterthought. In the Third Folio it's in with the tragedies, but some modern *Complete Works* place it in the comedies, despite its languidly unhappy ending. It lurches from tragedy to love story to comedy to satire, and back again. I've left it with the tragedies, purely because it needs to go somewhere and it's not exactly laugh a minute. Joyce Carol Oates, who has written widely about *Troilus*, describes it as 'tragedy of a special sort'.

## PLOT

The play is set during the war between the Greeks and the Trojans, and focuses more on the war than the love story of the title. Troilus, a Trojan prince, falls in love with Cressida, and gets her uncle Pandarus to fix it so they can meet. They pledge undying love and have one great night together, but sadly fate has other plans. Cressida's father, Calchas, has deserted to the Greek side. Wanting to see his daughter, he persuades the Greeks to exchange a Trojan prisoner of war for her. Prince Diomedes collects Cressida and takes her to the Greek camp; before you can say 'unfaithful', she's gone and fallen for him. Troilus is not happy, but at least this gets him all fired up for when the battle against the Greeks resumes.

The war, which incidentally was started by the Trojans when Prince Paris pinched beautiful Helen from her Greek hubby, has been going on for seven years. Agamemnon, the Greek General, asks Ulysses, one of his commanders, why the army is so listless. Ulysses explains they're taking their cue from Achilles, formerly the greatest of the Greek warriors, who now prefers to hang out with his lover Patroclus than to fight. When Troy issues a challenge that Hector, their best warrior, is willing to fight one-to-one, Ulysses chooses the foolish Ajax over Achilles for the job, in the hope that this rebuff will remind Achilles of his duties.

Hector and Ajax fight, and though Hector is at the point of victory he refuses to kill Ajax because he has realised that they're cousins. Hostilities resume the next day. When Hector kills Patroclus, Achilles is finally persuaded to return to battle.

He and some other Greek soldiers corner and kill Hector, and the Trojans retreat to their city to mourn. Finally we see Troilus again (remember him?). He takes Hector's place as warrior and vows that they will get revenge on Achilles. And so the war between Troy and Greece continues.

## IN A NUTSHELL

Troilus and Cressida fall in love, fall out of love, the Trojan war drags on.

## OTHER NOTABLE CHARACTERS

Thersites, a Greek soldier, who sees the worst in everybody – one of Shakespeare's bitterest clowns. Cassandra, a Trojan woman who's full of prophecies, including the prediction of Hector's death, but everyone thinks she's mad so she's ignored.

## BODY COUNT

Just two, despite it being a war: Patroclus and Hector.

## DID YOU KNOW?

❖ Shakespeare probably based the story on Homer's *Iliad*, and *Troylus and Criseyde*, a poem by Chaucer, amongst other works.

❖ The play was little performed until after World War One when its themes seemed to chime with a new cynicism about war.

❖ Goethe saw something significant in the play, saying that while *Macbeth* was the play which worked best on the stage, if you wanted to see 'Shakespeare's mind unfettered, read *Troilus and Cressida*, where he treats the materials of the Iliad after his own fashion.'

 QUOTABLE LINES

*'Time hath, my lord,*
*A wallet at his back, wherein he puts*
*Alms for oblivion, a great-sized monster*
*Of ingratitudes.'*

*'Thou sodden-witted lord, thou hast*
*in thy skull no more brain than*
*I have in mine elbows.'*
**(THERSITES BEING RUDE TO AJAX.)**

*'I am a bastard, too. I love bastards.*
*I am bastard begot, bastard instructed,*
*bastard in mind, bastard in valour,*
*in everything illegitimate.'*
**(THERSITES AGAIN – HE GETS ALL THE GOOD LINES.)**

*'The common curse of mankind,*
*folly and ignorance.'*

*'The end crowns all,*
*And that old common arbitrator Time*
*Will one day end it.'*

## CHAPTER SIX
# THE APOCRYPHAL PLAYS

There are a number of plays classed as 'apocrypha', which means 'writings not considered genuine'. These are plays which have had Shakespeare's name attached to them but are, for one reason or another, currently outside the main canon.

So, do we know for sure how many plays Shakespeare wrote? Of course we don't. Was it...

### THIRTY-SIX?

The original First Folio contained 36 plays.

### THIRTY-SEVEN?

*Pericles*
For a long time, the general consensus has been that Shakespeare wrote 37 plays, and that Pericles was mistakenly left out of the

First Folio. It was included in the Third Folio, but then so were six other plays, most of which are not widely regarded as being by Shakespeare.

If you Google the question, 'How many plays did Shakespeare write?', you usually get a qualified '37', which acknowledges that this might change, pending further evidence. In fact, this answer is out of date, because most scholars would definitely include the next two.

## THIRTY-EIGHT?

### The Two Noble Kinsmen

It's now generally accepted that The Two Noble Kinsmen, a collaboration with John Fletcher, should be in the canon. The Oxford Complete Works included it in 1986, and most other Complete Works now have it. So do I.

## THIRTY-NINE?

### Edward III

First attributed to Shakespeare in 1656, Edward III took a long time to be accepted as one of his collaborations (with Thomas Kyd). It was included in The Riverside Shakespeare in 1996 and in the 2005 edition of The Oxford Complete Works. It's sometimes credited to 'William Shakespeare and Others' as some people reckon it was written by a group of playwrights (including Kyd).

Thirty-nine is the number I've gone for in this book, in line with Andrew Dickson's The Globe Guide to Shakespeare (2016), but still the possible contenders keep coming...

## FORTY?

### Sir Thomas More

*The Oxford Complete Works* lists 40 plays (plus notes on two others). The additional play is *The Book of Sir Thomas More*, written around 1603, for which there's no record of publication or performance. Excitingly though, there is a manuscript of the play in the British Library written by several people, and one of those hands – Hand D – is believed to be that of Shakespeare. If true, it would be the only item we have in his handwriting, other than the signatures on his will and other legal documents. It would also be the only thing that gives us an insight into Shakespeare's editing process (a lot of crossing out, comfortingly).

Other possible playwrights who worked on *Sir Thomas More* include Anthony Munday, Henry Chettle, Thomas Dekker and Thomas Heywood, all of whom wrote for the Admiral's Men at some point. Shakespeare's contribution is believed to consist mainly of a dramatic speech spoken by More to a mob protesting against immigration. More asks them to think how they would feel, were they adrift in a foreign land. Very topical. The RSC produced *Sir Thomas More* in 2005; and in 2016, as part of their *Shakespeare Live!* event, Ian McKellen delivered this speech, suggesting that at least part of the play is moving towards full canon respectability.

## FORTY-ONE?

### Cardenio or Double Falsehood

Listed in *The Oxford Complete Works*, but only as a two-page 'brief account', *Cardenio* has a long and confusing history. Believed to be one of the late collaborations with John Fletcher, and concerning an episode from *Don Quixote* by Cervantes, it's long been regarded as lost. This play was mentioned in a number of contemporary records but has never turned up – it's one of those Shakespearean missing links one always hopes to find in a granny's attic (along with a well-preserved First Folio and a handwritten diary explaining what went on during the lost years).

However, a play called *Double Falsehood*, written by eighteenth-century dramatist Lewis Theobald, is believed to contain some or all of *Cardenio*. Theobald claimed to have based *Falsehood* on a lost Shakespeare play, though annoyingly he didn't say which one. In 2010, *The Arden Complete Works* surprised many by including *Double Falsehood*, though the editors did note that Shakespeare's involvement in the play wasn't completely confirmed and might be disproved in the future. The RSC performed a 'reconstructed' *Cardenio* in 2011, taking *Double Falsehood* as a starting point and adding some new scenes from *Don Quixote*, adapted by Spanish writer Antonio Alamo.

The play *The Second Maiden's Tragedy* has also been proposed as being the missing *Cardenio*, though it seems more likely to be a different play by Thomas Middleton.


## FORTY-TWO?

### *Love's Labour's Won*

Francis Meres, a peer of Shakespeare, included *Love's Labour's Won* in a contemporary list of Shakespeare's plays. This play has never been found, and is now generally regarded as the alternative name for a play we know well. Possible contenders are *Much Ado About Nothing*, *All's Well That Ends Well* or *The Taming of the Shrew*. Of course, it might still be uncovered sometime in that granny's attic... *The Oxford Complete Works* includes it, like *Cardenio*, as a 'brief account'.

## LOADS MORE?

You could spend years studying all the plays attributed to Shakespeare. Some might have been genuine collaborations with the man, while others perhaps just had his editorial input, rather like top screenwriters nowadays who are brought in to add a masterly gloss to a script that's not working. And others were just fibbingly said to be by Shakespeare, probably to fool punters that they were getting a quality play.

Here are a few of the notable others all still outside the canon.

### Third Folio Extras
The 1664 reissue of the Third Folio (first published in 1663) listed seven more plays than the First Folio. Of these, only *Pericles* has thus far been accepted into the fold. Of the others, *The London Prodigal* is generally regarded to have had a minor input from Shakespeare, possibly in terms of the rough plot, but was written by someone else. *Thomas Lord Cromwell* was unlikely to have had anything to do with Shakespeare, despite it being attributed to 'W.S.' (a different playwright, Wentworth Smith, seems much more likely); *Locrine* and *The Puritan* are both W.S. red herrings. *Sir John Oldcastle* was written, according to Philip Henslowe's contemporary notes, by Anthony Munday and others; and *A Yorkshire Tragedy* is most likely one of Thomas Middleton's.

### Other Possibles
Several more plays are said to have some (rather small) input from Shakespeare, though the jury of mainstream scholars is still very much out. These include *The Spanish Tragedy*, *Mucedorus* and *Arden of Faversham*. These just scrape the surface of the many excitable debates about who wrote what, but that seems plenty for now.

## CHAPTER SEVEN
# THE POETRY

Shakespeare was as prolific a poet as he was a playwright, producing 154 sonnets and four long poems in a relatively short space of time. The Sonnets are a modest 14 lines each, but the long poems are long. *Really* long. The four of them total more than 30,000 words – about the same as a novella such as *Of Mice and Men*. The long poems were Shakespeare's greatest success during his lifetime, though it's the Sonnets which have stood the test of time.

## THE SONNETS

The sonnet as a poetic form was briefly fashionable in the late sixteenth century, but by the time Shakespeare's were published in 1609 it was already falling out of favour. It might seem extraordinary when we read them now, but his weren't widely admired. However, a couple of hundred years after his death, their reputation started to build, and these days many people consider them the pinnacle of his literary achievements. Cole Porter's song 'You're the Top' includes the Sonnets in his list of the greatest things in the world (along with the Colosseum, the smile on the *Mona Lisa* and a Waldorf salad).

Shakespeare's Sonnets have long been the subject of intense fascination, and their power to generate interpretation is legendary. W. H. Auden commented, 'There has been more nonsense written about Shakespeare's Sonnets than about any other piece of literature extant.' One edition, published in 2000, comes with 400 additional pages of commentary and analysis, in which every poem is forensically examined and almost every line deconstructed.

The huge interest is partly because many of the poems are very lovely and romantic, but mainly because they seem so personal; there's always the hope that they're windows into the soul of the writer. Bill Bryson notes that the Sonnets have driven scholars crazy because they are 'so frankly confessional in tone and yet so opaque.' As with the plays, hundreds of years of speculation have created an awful lot of noise. But we still don't know a great deal for certain about the meanings behind the Sonnets.

## WHAT IS A SONNET?

There are various forms of sonnet, such as the Italian and Miltonic (named for John Milton). The type of sonnet Shakespeare wrote – English sonnets, now commonly known as Shakespearean sonnets – follow a few rules: 14 lines, each of ten syllables; with alternate lines rhyming, apart from the last two which rhyme with each other.

Thanks to Shakespeare, sonnets are now synonymous with love poetry. Indeed, in one of the greatest love scenes ever written, Romeo and Juliet speak in the form of a sonnet. Shakespeare's Sonnets muse on lust, beauty, jealousy, infidelity, lasting love, and much more on the timeless topic of love, but they also cover themes such as art, nature, eternity and death.

## WHICH ARE SHAKESPEARE'S MOST FAMOUS SONNETS?

### Sonnet 18

Perhaps the best known Sonnet begins 'Shall I compare thee to a summer's day?' It quickly goes on to say that the loved one is even better. For instance, one of the less appealing things about summer is that it's over all too quickly – unlike the lover, whose beauty is eternal. Ah, so romantic!

*Shall I compare thee to a summer's day?*
*Thou art more lovely and more temperate.*
*Rough winds do shake the darling buds of May,*
*And summer's lease hath all too short a date.*
*Sometime too hot the eye of heaven shines,*
*And often is his gold complexion dimmed,*
*And every fair from fair sometime declines,*
*By chance or nature's changing course untrimmed;*
*But thy eternal summer shall not fade*
*Nor lose possession of that fair thou ow'st,*
*Nor shall death brag thou wander'st in his shade*
*When in eternal lines to time thou grow'st.*
*So long as men can breathe or eyes can see,*
*So long lives this, and this gives life to thee.*

## DID YOU KNOW?

The phrase 'the darling buds of May' was borrowed by H. E. Bates for the title of his successful comic novels about the Larkin family, published in the 1950s.

## Sonnet 116

This poem is much loved by people looking for something to read at a wedding, as it not only mentions the word 'marriage' but also riffs around the theme of true love not fading over time. The first few lines always bring a tear to my eye. It begins:

> *Let me not to the marriage of true minds*
> *Admit impediments. Love is not love*
> *Which alters when it alteration finds,*
> *Or bends with the remover to remove.*
> *O no, it is an ever-fixèd mark*
> *That looks on tempests and is never shaken.*

## Sonnet 130

The narrator here compares his lover to various natural beauties, and finds her seriously lacking: her cheeks aren't the colour of roses nor her breath as sweet as perfume. Rude! Yet the last two lines show the true depth of his feelings towards her, saying she is as special as those described 'with false compare'. Some consider the final couplet scant recompense for a poem that comprehensively disses the lady but I think this is lovely, perhaps because I'm fond of a slightly cynical, backhanded compliment that expresses a genuine feeling. Here are the first few lines:

> *My mistress' eyes are nothing like the sun;*
> *Coral is far more red than her lips' red.*
> *If snow be white, why then her breasts are dun;*
> *If hairs be wires, black wires grow on her head.*

## Sonnet 73

The passing of time is a recurring theme in the Sonnets, perhaps most notably in this one, which is popular despite its melancholy musing on the nature of ageing and death. It starts:

> *That time of year thou mayst in me behold*
> *When yellow leaves, or none, or few, do hang*
> *Upon those boughs which shake against the cold,*
> *Bare ruined choirs where late the sweet birds sang.*
> *In me thou seest the twilight of such day*
> *As after sunset fadeth in the west,*
> *Which by and by black night doth take away,*
> *Death's second self, that seals up all in rest.*

The narrator feels insecure, sure that his younger friend notices the ravages of time on his face. He tries to explain how it feels to get old, for one day the young friend will experience the same thing. In concluding, Shakespeare determines that the only thing that matters, since we'll all age and die, is the strength of love. Ah, how wise! If a bit gloomy...

# SHAKESPEARE AND ME

*Jo Shapcott is an award-winning poet and her collections include* My Life Asleep *and* Of Mutability. *The Royal Society of Literature commissioned Jo to write a sonnet in reply to one of Shakespeare's.*

### What was your switch-on moment?

A production of *Henry IV, Part I* when I was 14. I vividly remember the play springing off the page. It was very exciting, and I was entranced by the language; but the bigger thing I remember is getting drunk in the grounds and being sick. So the second half was a blur. I fought with my boyfriend on the way home on the coach and got told off by my teachers. Shakespeare got tied in with sex and alcohol in my mind, leaving behind a heady coming-of-age memory. It seems appropriate as *Henry IV* features a reprobate [Falstaff].

### Which is your favourite of Shakespeare's poems?

Sonnet 73. It's about ageing, and it's gorgeous. I love its series of correctives, none of them quite right. 'When yellow leaves, or none, or few...' Which is it? We never know. The syntax, particularly in the second half, is brilliant. The way he subverts the rhythm, like a jazz improviser, but never loses sight of it completely. It's all of that and more.

**Tell us about the most memorable performance you've seen.**

*Midsummer Night's Dream* in London. I was young, 17, and it's about young love. And transformation. It's no coincidence that transformation is the backbone of everything I've written – you can trace it back there to that performance.

**Which Shakespeare character would you most like to meet?**

The Fool in *King Lear*. I have characters in my poetry who are related to the idea of the wise fool. They access a different kind of reality through their spongy minds. *Lear* is my favourite play. It has it all. The language, the imagery, ageing, madness, the terror of the old man losing everything. I always cry when I see it.

**How would you persuade somebody to give Shakespeare a chance?**

Often it's about undoing bad teaching. But the key is to read it aloud. People get put off by the look of the language, but if you say it out loud, play with the way the words sound, you'll be able to follow the thinking in them. And then you will have direct contact with a mind working centuries ago, which is amazing.

## OTHER NOTABLE SONNETS

❖ Sonnet 20 compares the beloved's beauty to both a man and a woman's: 'A woman's face with nature's own hand painted / Hast thou, the master-mistress of my passion'. In modern English, this would run something like: 'Nature gave you a face as pretty as a woman's / You are both the master and mistress of my love.' The phrase 'master-mistress' has been picked over feverishly by many hundreds, if not thousands, of keen-eyed scholars in a hopeless attempt to pin down Shakespeare's unknowable sexuality.

❖ Sonnet 29, which begins, 'When, in disgrace with fortune and men's eyes, / I all alone beweep my outcast state', has been turned into a song by Rufus Wainwright, referenced by T. S. Eliot in his poem *Ash Wednesday,* read out to Julia Roberts by Richard Gere in *Pretty Woman*, and quoted in *Star Trek: The Next Generation.*

❖ Sonnet 33, which starts, 'Full many a glorious morning have I seen', is mostly interpreted as an expression of regret that the narrator and the beloved are somewhat estranged. However, it has also been suggested that it refers to Shakespeare's son Hamnet, who died in childhood: 'But out, alack, he was but one hour mine.'

❖ Sonnet 93 was the first of Shakespeare's works to be subjected to a biographical analysis. Edmond Malone, an early scholar of Shakespeare, proposed in 1780 that the Sonnet might reveal the unhappy state of Shakespeare's marriage. It begins: 'So shall I live supposing thou art true / Like a deceivèd husband'. Malone bolstered his interpretation of husbandly jealousy by pointing to the apparent snub of the 'second best bed' in the will. He backtracked even as he speculated, clearly recognising that he was crossing a line: 'The whole is mere conjecture.' But it was too late; the door to biographical interpretations opened, and the world rushed in. Modern Shakespeare professor James Shapiro cites this as a turning point in the study of art and literature – the moment 'scholarship had stumbled off course'.

❖ Sonnets 135 and 136 play with the word 'will', using it 19 times across the two poems, in a variety of different meanings. Sonnet 136 concludes, 'And then thou lov'st me for my name is Will.' Interpretations are boundless.

❖ Sonnet 138 is a classic poem about the lies lovers tell: 'When my love swears that she is made of truth / I do believe her though I know she lies'. But it's their fibs, the poet reckons, that keep them together: 'Therefore I lie with her, and she with me'. This has a cheeky double meaning, for it can mean telling lies, or – ahem – lying down with each other.

❖ Sonnet 145 has what looks like a pun on Anne Hathaway's name, suggesting it was written as a love poem directly to her: '"I hate" from hate away she threw'.

## WHAT ARE THE SONNETS ABOUT?

They fall into three groups.

### 1. The Fair Youth
Most of them – the first 126 – are addressed to a 'you', who's known variously as 'my lovely boy', 'lovely youth', 'beauteous and lovely boy'. They're usually referred to as the 'Fair Youth Poems', though that exact phrase doesn't appear in the Sonnets. Most of the poems are expressions of romantic love, and all that

involves: jealousy, anxiety, mistrust – and, ultimately, of an affair between the youth and the narrator's Dark Lady.

Contained within these poems are a handful known as the 'Rival Poet Sonnets', in which the narrator chides the Fair Youth for his interest in another poet. You may be sure that the possible identity of this rival has been thoroughly examined (candidates include Christopher Marlowe, George Chapman and Samuel Daniel), though no conclusion has been reached.

## 2. The Dark Lady

The next 26 Sonnets are about a woman with black hair, known (though not in the Sonnets themselves) as the Dark Lady. These poems explore sexual love more explicitly than most of those to the young man, and also cover less flattering concerns, in which she's accused of deceit and infidelity. Some of the Sonnets are deliberately insulting, blaming the woman for the lust she incites.

## 3. Cupid Poems

The final two Sonnets are little scenes featuring Cupid, and they're addressed to neither the young man nor the Dark Lady.

## ADDRESSED TO A MAN, DID YOU SAY?

The theory that Shakespeare was gay can be traced back to the Fair Youth Poems. These poems – some tender, some passionate, some downright erotic – have caused much consternation and hand-wringing over the centuries. The second edition of the Sonnets, published in 1640, changed some of the hes to shes, sidestepping any unpleasantness that might have offended seventeenth-century sensibilities.

## SO WAS SHAKESPEARE GAY?

The short answer is that we don't know. The longer answer goes something like this:

❖ Possibly. Or at least bisexual, as he was married to a woman. Male sexuality was apparently a fairly ambiguous thing back then. Still is, some might say. And homosexuality wasn't really a concept in the way we understand it now.

❖ Possibly not, as the first 17 'Procreation Sonnets' all urge the young man to get married. While some of the encouragement is so the Fair Youth can pass on his beauty to his children, at the very least it's a bit confusing.

❖ Possibly, though we don't know if the 126 poems are addressed to the same man, or indeed whether many of them are addressed to a man at all. Some certainly are, but it's only because we regard them as a sequence that we assume they're a great outpouring to the same fellow. They may well have been written over a number of years to a lot of different friends and/or lovers.

❖ Possibly not, because many of the poems can be read as being to a good friend rather than a sexual love object. Certainly, a lot of anxiously homophobic interpretations have taken that line.

❖ Possibly, because some of the Sonnets can also be read, as Andrew Dickson puts it, as being 'surprisingly frank about the appeals – and difficulties' of homosexuality. Sonnet 20, for instance, contains teasing allusions that the narrator wishes to share more than just a lovely friendship with the Fair Youth. Poet Don Paterson points out that being in love with a man is a reasonable measure of homosexuality, and if Shakespeare wasn't in love with a man he was certainly brilliant at getting inside the head of someone who was.

❖ Possibly not, because we have no evidence whatsoever that the poems are in any way autobiographical. (See the next section.)

## ARE THE SONNETS AUTOBIOGRAPHICAL?

The Sonnets are all written in the first person, which has led many people to assume that they are therefore factual accounts. However, as with all works in which the author makes use of the first person, the 'I' doesn't have to be Shakespeare's own self. Writers are adept at imagining how it feels to be someone else, and trying out different personae. A crime writer doesn't have to have committed murder in order to imagine how it feels, and a poet doesn't have to be passionately in love to write as though they are.

'I am not the I of my novels,' says author Howard Jacobson as he advises against reading the Sonnets as if they were a record of Shakespeare's life. W. H. Auden, ever ready to caution against interpretation, counselled would-be biographers of the Sonnets that it is 'nonsensical to waste time trying to identify characters. It is an idiot's job, pointless and uninteresting.' Everyone nodded, then pretty much ignored him.

Admittedly, biographical interpretations were muted for a long time because of the whole 'lovely boy' business being a bit of a facer for those who couldn't countenance the thought of the world's greatest playwright being gay. But by the middle of the nineteenth century, James Shapiro says, 'the obsession with autobiographical titbits had all but displaced interest in the aesthetic pleasures of the poems themselves.'

Wordsworth was a strong advocate of the notion that Shakespeare revealed his true self in the Sonnets. In his own poem 'Scorn not the Sonnet', he wrote that 'with this key / Shakespeare unlocked his heart'. Robert Browning vehemently disagreed with Wordsworth in *his* poem, 'House': 'If so, the less Shakespeare he!'

The question of how much you can tell about someone from their writing is one we'll return to in the last chapter, where the claim that someone else wrote Shakespeare's plays is considered in more detail.

Now that Jacobson, Auden, Browning and I have all strongly urged caution, I'll plunge headlong into an exploration of the various autobiographical debates.

## THE FAMOUS DEDICATION

When the Sonnets were first published in 1609, the dedication at the front, signed by publisher Thomas Thorpe, read as follows:

> *TO.THE.ONLIE.BEGETTER.OF.*
> *THESE.INSUING.SONNETS.*
> *Mr.W.H.   ALL.HAPPINESSE.*
> *AND.THAT.ETERNITIE.*
> *PROMISED.*
> *BY.*
> *OUR.EVER-LIVING.POET.*
> *WISHETH.*
> *THE.WELL-WISHING.*
> *ADVENTURER.IN.*
> *SETTING.*
> *FORTH.*
>
> *T.T.*

This crazily cryptic dedication has intrigued scholars for hundreds of years, and we still don't know what it means. That Thorpe, rather than Shakespeare, signed the dedication is often considered to be evidence that the work was published without permission. It's not known how Thorpe came to have the poems, and it's been speculated that Shakespeare meant the Sonnets to be private, for friends only, and wasn't pleased when they turned up in a book.

The dedication raises three questions:

1. What exactly *is* an 'onlie begetter' when it's at home?
2. Who was Mr W.H.?
3. Was he the same person as the Fair Youth to whom so many poems are addressed?

### What is an 'Onlie Begetter'?

'Onlie begetter' has long been assumed to mean either the person who acquired the poems from Shakespeare, or the person who inspired them. The latter has led many people to assume that Mr W.H. was one and the same as the Fair Youth.

### Who Was Mr W.H.? Was He the Fair Youth?

For years, it was believed that the poems addressed to the Fair Youth were written for a patron, or someone Shakespeare was hoping would become a patron. They contain rather fawning language, and words such as 'your servant' and 'duty'. Assuming the Fair Youth, a patron and Mr W.H. are one and the same, there are only two feasible candidates: Henry Wriothesley, 3rd Earl of Southampton, and William Herbert, 3rd Earl of Pembroke.

Both had some kind of patronage relationship with Shakespeare; two of his long poems are addressed to Wriothesley, while Herbert was a dedicatee of the First Folio. Wriothesley was undoubtedly a fair if not flamboyant youth, apparently as keen on men as women, and not averse to having his portrait painted while wearing a frock. Both men initially resisted marriage: Wriothesley paid a huge fine to get out of one engagement, while Herbert went to prison for refusing to wed Mary Fitton, one of the Queen's maids of honour, after getting her pregnant. So the poems urging the youth to marry would make sense for either candidate. Sure, only Herbert's initials were the right way round for W.H., but Wriothesley's are easily reversed. However, what puts paid to either of them being Mr W.H. is that publisher Thomas Thorpe would never have referred to noble lords as 'Mr'.

Shakespeare scholar Jonathan Bate believes that the Fair Youth and Mr W.H. need to be separated. He thinks the Fair Youth was most likely Henry Wriothesley, and that the poems were written for him in the quest for patronage.

Many other – non-noble – candidates for Mr W.H. have been proposed, including William Harvey, Wriothesley's stepfather; William Hall, a printer; William Hart, Shakespeare's nephew; and even William Himself (i.e. Shakespeare), this last theory in particular accompanied by the distinct sound of barrel-scraping.

One recent theory proposes a publisher called William Holme as W.H. Holme had connections to Thomas Thorpe, and died two years before the Sonnets were published, which might explain the slightly elegiac wording of the dedication. Perhaps Holme was the begetter of the poems in that he procured them and passed them to Thorpe?

Maybe. Maybe not. There is one other possible answer. 'Begetter' may have meant 'author'. If Thorpe hadn't mentioned Mr W.H., we would have assumed the dedication was to Shakespeare himself because it reads like an acknowledgement of the author. So there's an almost comically straightforward explanation: 'Mr W.H.' could be meant to say 'Mr W.S.' (Mr William Shakespeare). A printer might have mistaken Thorpe's handwritten S for an H;

'secretary hand', a style of writing at the time, has a version in which capitals S and H are extremely similar.

As Jonathan Bate puts it, sounding as if he's sniggering slightly, 'Might the mysterious Mr W.H.... be no more than an inky slip, the creation of a misprint?'

---

### DID YOU KNOW?

Oscar Wilde wrote a story called *The Portrait of Mr W.H.*, in which the eponymous fellow is a handsome boy actor called Willie Hughes. Wilde presumably wasn't averse to the notion that Shakespeare might have been interested in men.

---

## WHO WAS THE DARK LADY?

There has been frenzied speculation over the identity of the Dark Lady, the focus of 26 of the Sonnets. Over the years, she has variously been proposed as: Mary Fitton, Queen Elizabeth's maid and mistress of William Herbert (though she was apparently fair-haired); Aemilia Lanyer, the first Englishwoman to publish her own poems, who was of Jewish-Venetian origin and possibly dark-skinned; Elizabeth Wriothesley, wife of Henry; and Lucy Morgan, a prostitute, sometimes known as Lucy Negro or Black Luce (she at least would have had the correct colouring). Shakespeare's descriptions of the Dark Lady's hair as 'black wires', her eyes as 'raven black' and her 'dun' breast (meaning dusky) are strongly suggestive of a black woman rather than a white woman with dark hair.

The most recent possible contender, proposed originally by Jonathan Bate, is Aline Florio, wife of John Florio, who was Henry Wriothesley's language tutor. Little is known of her, other than that she was the sister of poet Samuel Daniel. However, Bate has lately come to mock his own theory, saying he'd fallen into the seductive trap of projecting 'a story of my own into their [the poems'] narrative.'

---

### DID YOU KNOW?

The Dark Lady has been a popular subject for writers. George Bernard Shaw wrote a play called *The Dark Lady of the Sonnets*; Sally O'Reilly's novel *Dark Aemilia* brings to life Aemilia Lanyer's alleged relationship with Shakespeare; and Victoria Lamb has penned a series of historical romances about Lucy Morgan.

---

# THE LONG POEMS

Shakespeare wrote four long poems (we think): *Venus and Adonis*, *The Rape of Lucrece*, *A Lover's Complaint* and *The Phoenix and the Turtle*. The first three are narrative poems, meaning simply that they tell a story; they all still rhyme. The last one is an allegorical poem with a symbolic, underlying meaning.

*Venus and Adonis* and *The Rape of Lucrece* were written during 1592–94, years when theatres were closed owing to the plague. Shakespeare probably had time on his hands, and a pressing need to earn some money. Both poems opened with ingratiating dedications to Henry Wriothesley, presumably in the hope that he'd send a few groats Shakespeare's way.

## VENUS AND ADONIS

*Venus and Adonis* was the greatest success of Shakespeare's career, by far the most popular thing he published during his lifetime. The story, based on Ovid's poem *Metamorphoses*, concerns Venus, the goddess of love, pursuing the handsome young mortal Adonis. He isn't much interested; nonetheless they share a passionate moment, after which she chases him round, and there's absolutely loads of kissing. He isn't all that into her, and just wants to get back to hunting, but when he does, he's mortally wounded. Venus is devastated when she stumbles upon his bloodstained body.

The poem is comic in tone, and also rather racy, with descriptions of female sexual desire that must have read like soft porn to a thrilled Elizabethan audience. This kind of long storytelling poem was just becoming popular. Christopher Marlowe's long poem *Hero and Leander* was published shortly after, and was also wildly successful.

*Venus and Adonis* contains memorably bouncy lines like:

*'desire doth lend her force
Courageously to pluck him from his horse'*

### AND

*'She red and hot as coals of glowing fire;
He red for shame, but frosty in desire.'*

## *THE RAPE OF LUCRECE*

This poem, published a year later, in 1594, was considerably longer than *Venus and Adonis*. Indeed, at 1,855 lines, it was longer than *The Comedy of Errors*. It tells the story of Tarquin, who sets his mind on raping the virtuous Lucrece as she lies sleeping. Mind you, he does a lot of agonising about it first:

> *'What win I if I gain the thing I seek?*
> *A dream, a breath, a froth of fleeting joy.*
> *Who buys a minute's mirth to wail a week,*
> *Or sells eternity to get a toy?'*

Once the terrible act is done, Lucrece is tormented with guilt – in a horribly realistic way – and ultimately kills herself. Hmm, it might be possible to see why it wasn't quite as successful as Shakespeare's earlier poem.

### DID YOU KNOW?

The two long poems' dedications to Henry Wriothesley are just about the only occasions we know of when Shakespeare speaks directly to us in his own voice. Naturally, they've been analysed to death. All we can really say for sure is that Shakespeare spoke very fondly of the young earl: 'The love I dedicate to your lordship is without end' and 'What I have done is yours; what I have to do is yours; being part in all I have, devoted yours.'

## A LOVER'S COMPLAINT

It's not known when this poem was written, but it was first published in 1609, at the end of the book of Sonnets. There has long been debate about whether it's definitely by Shakespeare. It wasn't till the 1960s that it was officially considered one of his, though there's still dissent now. Many feel that if it *was* Shakespeare's, it wasn't exactly his finest hour. However, others disagree, finding a brilliant truthfulness in the descriptions of obsessive feelings.

The story is of a young woman complaining about having been seduced and dumped by a handsome chap, the sort who's attractive to everyone: 'sexes both enchanted'. She chucks the cad's letters and gifts into the river, and tells a passing old man all her woes. She concludes by saying that, despite everything, she'd probably fall for him again if he were to turn up ('And new pervert a reconcilèd maid.'), showing an impressive level of cool-eyed self-knowledge.

## THE PHOENIX AND THE TURTLE

This poem, an allegory about – possibly – the ideal marriage and the death of love, is generally regarded as one of Shakespeare's most enigmatic pieces of writing. It's not widely admired and is often not mentioned at all; Andrew Dickson's otherwise comprehensive *Rough Guide to Shakespeare* gives it a scant couple of lines. Some people do rate it more highly, however.

It was published in 1601 as part of a collection of poems called *Love's Martyr*, written by various people including Ben Jonson. The same theme runs through all the poems: that of the love between the legendary phoenix and the turtle dove, a symbol of fidelity (the turtle of the title refers to the bird, not the slow-moving reptile). Shakespeare's comparatively short poem (67 lines) focuses on the last part of the story, when the lovebirds kill themselves by burning together in the phoenix's flames.

Interpreters of this odd poem have pondered whether the chaste relationship between the phoenix and the turtle dove represents that of Queen Elizabeth and her close friend Sir John Salusbury; or her relationship with the Earl of Essex, which ended in his execution for plotting to overthrow her. Alternatively, some who believe that Shakespeare was a closet Catholic think it might be a commemoration of a Catholic martyr called Anne Line, executed in 1601, and her husband, Roger.

## DID YOU KNOW?

Shakespeare has been proposed as the author of a number of other poems, including 'Shall I Die?' and 'A Funeral Elegy'. The current evidence largely weighs against these being by him.

## CHAPTER EIGHT
# SHAKESPEARE'S INFLUENCE

*Fantastic! And it was all written with a feather!*
**ATTRIBUTED TO SAM GOLDWYN, HOLLYWOOD FILM MOGUL**

## PART ONE
# EVERYBODY LOVES SHAKESPEARE
### (OK, NOT *EVERYBODY*)

In 2016, the 400th anniversary of Shakespeare's death, the celebrations confirmed that his popularity shows no sign of waning. On the contrary. Hundreds of events celebrating the writer and his work took place all over the world, including the tour of a precious First Folio across America to every state; a major RSC tour of China; a five-day Shakespeare festival in Alexandria, Egypt; performances of short versions of the plays in New Delhi, India; a pop-up Globe in Auckland, New Zealand; and a visit by the Chandos portrait to Moscow, Russia. There were also hundreds of events in Shakespeare's homeland, particularly in London and Stratford-upon-Avon, from parades, performances and President Obama visiting the Globe, to live events beamed from the RSC into cinemas and on the BBC.

His plays are constantly being performed all over the world; he's never off the school curriculum; he's been reimagined through the lens of hip-hop, ballet, Bollywood, manga, opera, Japanese Noh theatre, puppets and graphic novels; and his work has been translated into more than a hundred languages, from Korean and Arabic to Esperanto and Klingon.

The man still got it.


## THIS VAST ILLUMINATION

What *is* it about Shakespeare? His plays entertain us, for sure, but his appeal is because they have always done so much more than just entertain. They hold up a mirror, showing what it is to be us, in all our beautiful, flawed, complicated humanity. What's more, the plays are endlessly adaptable to time, place and circumstance, changing their meaning depending on when and where they're performed. His characters speak our hidden thoughts out loud, shining a light on envy, love, ambition and hate. The plays understand friendship, marriage and parenthood, the impetuousness of young love and the indignities of old age. And – no small thing – the language is often instantly memorable, the phrases ringing in our ears long after we've read or heard the words.

## EVERYBODY LOVES SHAKESPEARE

Well, not quite everyone – George Bernard Shaw and Tolstoy, I'm looking at you. But over the last four centuries, just about everyone has had something to say about him, mostly nice.

Ben Jonson, Shakespeare's friend and rival, kicked off the whole love-in with his poem 'To the Memory of My Beloved the Author, Mr. William Shakespeare'. Printed at the start of the First Folio in 1623, this contained the immortal, much-quoted line: 'He was not of an age but for all time!' How prescient this turned out to be: a seventeenth-century prediction of Shakespeare's astonishing ability to be relevant to every era and every place.

In *Mansfield Park*, Jane Austen has Henry Crawford say, in a quote often attributed as Jane's own view: 'Shakespeare… is a part of an Englishman's constitution. His thoughts and beauties are so spread abroad that one touches them everywhere; one is intimate with him by instinct.'

But you don't have to be British to feel that way. Flaubert, the quintessential Frenchman, said, 'When I read Shakespeare I become greater, wiser, purer.' And the Dutch Van Gogh, writing to his brother in 1889, spoke for many of us when he explained how the work made him feel: 'What touches me… is that the voices of these people, which… reach us from a distance of several centuries, do not seem unfamiliar to us. It is so much alive that you think you know them and see the thing.'

Others have unfavourably compared the great outpouring of Shakespeare-inspired commentary with the man's own work. Such as nineteenth-century writer William Hazlitt, who said, 'If we wish to know the force of human genius, we should read Shakespeare. If we wish to see the insignificance of human learning, we may study his commentators.' (I'll try not to take that personally.)

Still others have marvelled over Shakespeare's extraordinary longevity and influence. In her diary of 1934, Virginia Woolf reflected on visiting Shakespeare's grave: 'down there one foot from me lay the little bones that had spread over the world this vast illumination.'

## NOT EVERYBODY LOVES SHAKESPEARE

French writer Voltaire described *Hamlet* as: 'A coarse and barbarous piece, which would not be tolerated by the lowest rabble of France and Italy... You would suppose it to be a product of a drunken savage.' Leo Tolstoy was, if that's possible, even less keen: 'I remember the astonishment I felt when I first read Shakespeare. I expected to receive a powerful aesthetic pleasure, but... not only did I feel no delight, but I felt an irresistible repulsion and tedium.' Mind you, he hated Chekhov too ('worse than Shakespeare'), hinting that Tolstoy the great novelist was perhaps less astute as a literary critic. George Orwell, 40 years later, suggested that the source of Tolstoy's animosity was his Christian ideals, which clashed with Shakespeare's exuberant humanity.

Lewis Carroll loved the plays, but hated what he regarded as the profanity of much of the language. Amongst the papers discovered after Carroll's death in 1898, there was a plan to create a sanitised version of the *Complete Works*, suitable for children – presumably, specifically for Alice 'In Wonderland' Liddell. Henry James also valued the plays (in an 1876 review of *Romeo and Juliet*, he said, 'One never sees Shakespeare played without being reminded at some new point of his greatness'), but seemed offended at the thought of a pleb from Stratford as their writer. John Bailey recorded in his diary James's clashing views of Shakespeare: 'the works on the one side and, on the other, that dull face, and all the stories we know of the man: "commonplace; commonplace; almost degrading."'

Charles Darwin wasn't a fan either: 'I have tried lately to read Shakespeare, and found it so intolerably dull that it nauseated me.'

Well, no one can please all the people all of the time. Maybe you too aren't keen. Perhaps you were put off by a bad experience at school. Sitting on a hard wooden chair, sniggering at Bottom's name (that can't *just* have been me, surely). Or perhaps having to learn long, incomprehensible speeches by heart. Maybe Shakespeare for you is clouded by that feeling one sometimes gets that he's Very Important And Serious And Will Do You Good in the way cod liver oil used to do kids good. But back in his day, Shakespeare was a supreme mass entertainer whose work was loved by people with little education. There is nothing in the plays that designates them as high intellectual art. I've mostly restrained myself from speculating about what Shakespeare would think if he was alive today, but can't help wondering what he'd make of the reverence with which his words – probably often dashed off to meet a deadline, a few loose ends still dangling – are now regarded. I'm sure he knew he was good. But *that* good?

Maybe you were taken to see an inferior production without anyone explaining the plot to you. I still think back to a wretched *Romeo and Juliet* when I was 14 that nearly tipped me over the edge into hatred for the poor playwright, but it wasn't his fault.

Perhaps you just don't get what all the fuss is about. Well, that's fine. Despite what we're sometimes led to believe, there's no law that says we have to like Shakespeare. But if you've got this far with the book, maybe you *want* to get him. Maybe you've listened to people go on about him, and are starting to suspect that they can't all be faking it. But this isn't 'one size fits all'. The thing that switched them on to Shakespeare won't be the same thing that'll work for you. Most of the interviewees in this book describe the moment when a line in a play or poem, or a great performance, spoke to them, right to the heart. Mine was watching Antony Sher fling himself about the stage on crutches, but, celebrated a performance as that was, not everyone who saw it felt as I did. Your switch-on moment, if it comes, will be different.

## SHAKESPEARE – THE LESS FABULOUS YEARS

No one at the time of his death would have bet on Shakespeare developing a reputation as the greatest English playwright. He was certainly well regarded, but Ben Jonson, John Fletcher and Francis Beaumont were far more popular. Beaumont died the same year as Shakespeare and was given a fulsome send-off and a grave in Westminster Abbey. Considerably more eulogies were written for dramatist William Cartwright (no, me neither), who died in 1643, than for Shakespeare.

Although many of Shakespeare's plays were regularly performed throughout the seventeenth century, plenty were not. *As You Like It*, for instance, wasn't seen on stage until 1723, 100 years after it was published, and *Troilus and Cressida* wasn't performed in its original form until the twentieth century. The Sonnets were forgotten for almost two centuries, while even the once-popular long poems were neglected.

## HIS RISING REPUTATION

The tide began to turn in the late eighteenth century. Jonathan Bate describes the shift thus: 'In 1700, Shakespeare was an admired dramatist... by 1800 he had become England's chief cultural icon.' An influential new edition of the plays, edited by Dr Samuel Johnson, came out in 1765, with a good set of explanatory notes which made them accessible.

But the major catalyst for the shift was David Garrick, the greatest actor-producer of the day. He adored Shakespeare and did more than anyone to put him on the map; though he was probably responsible for starting the cult of 'bardolatry' (excessive worship of Shakespeare). Garrick sometimes played fast and loose with the plays – his *King Lear* had a happy ending, and his version of *The Winter's Tale* was missing three of its five acts (to be fair, it might not have made a great deal less sense than when it was whole). But Garrick's three-day Shakespeare festival in Stratford in 1769 kick-started an upswing in Shakespeare's reputation that gathered pace like a snowball rolling down a mountain. It also sealed the fate of Stratford-upon-Avon as a tourist mecca, bringing hundreds of London types to this hitherto unknown country town. With Garrick's line-in-the-sand declaration during the festival, ''Tis he! 'Tis he! The god of our idolatry!', Shakespeare was firmly established as a genius of divine inspiration.

## DID YOU KNOW?

❖ A mulberry tree in the front garden of New Place, allegedly planted by Shakespeare himself, was cut down and sold in the 1750s. Items made from it, such as cups and boxes, sold like hot cakes during Garrick's festival and gained a status rather like religious relics.

❖ Alexandre Dumas, French author of *The Count of Monte Cristo* and *The Three Musketeers*, continued the divine theme started by Garrick: 'After God, Shakespeare has created most'. Laurence Olivier later took up the mantle: 'Shakespeare – the nearest thing in incarnation to the eye of God.'

## THE AUTHORSHIP QUESTION

You'd think there would be few downsides to being considered a divine genius, but the concept of genius makes some people rather cynical. They start looking at things a bit more closely, and ask questions. This is all reasonable. Then some people go all narrow-eyed and suspicious. This leads us to the biggest controversy surrounding Shakespeare, which rumbles on even today.

It seems that no one had any doubts during his life that Shakespeare was the author of the plays credited to him. No one voiced any uncertainty for pretty much 200 years after he died. But whether because Garrick and others began comparing him to God and declared his work to be High Art, or for some other reason, a few people became bothered by his humble origins. Notably, a nineteenth-century American woman, Delia Bacon, proposed philosopher and scientist Francis Bacon (no relation) as the true genius behind the works. Her resulting book was universally derided, and poor Delia ended her days in a psychiatric institution. Somehow, though, the idea took hold, and people such as Mark Twain and Henry James announced themselves as Baconians. One should never underestimate how much people love a conspiracy theory. Pretty soon, Francis Bacon, who had been busy enough in life with his own work and was well documented as someone who thought the theatre frivolous, was apparently the author not just of Shakespeare's plays, but of those by Marlowe, Kyd and others. J. M. Barrie, the author of *Peter Pan*, once wittily commented, 'I know not, sir, whether Bacon wrote the works of Shakespeare, but if he did not it seems to me that he missed the opportunity of his life.'

Over the years many people have been proposed as the real author of the plays. The Shakespearean Authorship Trust (a group described by myth-busting website **snopes.com** as 'seemingly determined to credit Shakespeare's work to anyone but Shakespeare himself') offer – straight-faced – 66 possible alternatives. Candidates include Sir Walter Raleigh; William Stanley, 6th Earl of Derby; Mary Sidney Herbert, Countess of Pembroke; Sir Henry Neville; Edmund Spenser; and Queen Elizabeth. You'll notice that most of these are titled, though the non-noble Christopher Marlowe was a popular candidate for a while. At least he had the necessary writing chops, and the purists were pleased that he'd been to university. Unfortunately, he died in 1593, before the majority of Shakespeare's most famous plays appeared. Marlowe proponents' answer to this was that his death was faked, and he hid away for the next 20 years, writing plays under someone else's name. Of course he did.

The most popular alternative author for the so-called 'Anti-Stratfordian movement' is Edward de Vere, the 17th Earl of Oxford. He was undoubtedly well educated and even wrote a bit (though the works he produced wouldn't have given Shakespeare sleepless nights). Like Marlowe, Oxford's candidacy was fatally weakened by his untimely death, in 1604. Many of the later plays contain allusions to events which took place after this date. *Macbeth*, for instance, was clearly influenced by the Gunpowder Plot of 1605. Despite this small awkwardness, today there are still Oxfordians who believe that the Earl cleverly left a pile of plays ready to distribute at spaced-out intervals, with up-to-date references added to them by other people.

Whatever the shortcomings of the other candidates, the interesting question is why people *need* an alternative author to Shakespeare. Broadly, there are three key arguments put forward by supporters of the Anti-Stratfordian position.

## Argument 1: Shakespeare Wasn't Well Connected Enough to Have Written the Plays

Talk to an Anti-Stratfordian and sooner or later you stumble over a thinly disguised piece of snobbery: namely, that a provincial man who didn't go to university and who wasn't part of the royal court couldn't have written learned plays. A number of Shakespeare's contemporaries, such as Robert Greene and Thomas Nashe (the 'university wits'), did have a higher education. But others, such as Ben Jonson, did not, though no one ever suggests that this most intellectual of playwrights didn't write his own plays.

Shakespeare wasn't brought up in a deprived backwater. His father was high bailiff of a substantial town, and children from his background were able to get a decent classical education at grammar school. He needn't have been at court, or travelled, to imagine what that might be like. He could have read about these things in books, or spoken to people who knew about them. Or just made stuff up, as writers are wont to do.

The plays also make plenty of reference to rural concepts and ideas. One of the reasons Shakespeare was mocked by Robert Greene (of 'upstart crow' fame) is that he didn't try to hide his provincial underpinnings. It's not impossible for someone from a modest background to go on to great things. Abraham Lincoln, Charles Dickens, Vincent Van Gogh and Barack Obama spring to mind.

## Argument 2: There Is No Documentary Evidence of Shakespeare as an Author

Some Anti-Stratfordians claim that there are no sixteenth-century references to Shakespeare in the context of writing, but this is just malarkey. Contemporary writers such as Richard Greene, John Webster and Francis Meres referred to him as the author of plays and poems, and he's named as author all over the place: in the 1609 edition of the Sonnets; in the long poems *Venus and Adonis* and *The Rape of Lucrece*; in a number of quarto editions of the plays; and in the First Folio. In the accounts of the Master of the Revels (the record of plays performed before the King) for 1604–05, Shakespeare is named seven times as the author of plays performed.

If you've read this far, you'll be aware that we don't know as much as we would like about Shakespeare. But we know an awful lot more about him in relation to his writing than we do about anyone else. There are plenty of historical records connecting him to his work, but nothing connecting anyone else to it. Many Anti-Stratters simply say 'Aha!' (in the manner of whipping out a trump card) before advancing Argument Three.

## Argument 3: Shakespeare Was a Decoy

The Anti-Stratfordian answer to the frequent identification of Shakespeare in the historical record is that he was just a stand-in for the true playwright, and all those mentions of him are a con. He was, apparently, an 'amiable stooge' (a wry term used by Bill Bryson), who allowed his name to be used so that a shy and presumably noble playwright could get his plays out without being identified. As well as being bafflingly odd, this would have required the most extraordinary conspiracy, in which dozens, if not hundreds, of actors, writers, publishers and government officials would have had to keep a vow of silence.

Ultimately, the notion that Shakespeare was someone else is based on no evidence whatsoever. For a thorough account of the debate, the definitive work is James Shapiro's book *Contested Will*.

---

### DID YOU KNOW?

It's said that the statue which sits above Shakespeare's grave originally depicted him holding a sack of grain, a nod both to his roots as a country lad and to his later-life interests of grain-hoarding and -selling. But during the 'divinity years' of the late eighteenth century, this was regarded as *not at all* the thing, and the grain sack was replaced by a quill.

---

# PART TWO

# SHAKESPEARE'S INFLUENCE ON CULTURE

It's hard to think of someone who's had more influence on culture than Our Man from Stratford. So this section, which could run to 20 volumes, will be selective – if not downright biased – and will probably miss out your favourites.

## LITERATURE

Countless writers have been influenced by Shakespeare; sometimes overtly, basing plots or characters on his; but more often indirectly, by his use of language, his ability to inhabit the personae of males and females, young and old, poor and wealthy, kind and mean, and the way he made us think about our humanity. We have no way of knowing what literature would have looked like had he not existed, but most subsequent writers owe him a debt, one way or another.

## Novels

Many authors have acknowledged Shakespeare's influence, including Walter Scott, Charlotte Brontë, Oscar Wilde, Anton Chekhov, Rudyard Kipling, Marcel Proust, James Joyce, Boris Pasternak and Jorge Luis Borges.

His influence is present in such varied works as:

- ❖ *Moby Dick* by Herman Melville (shades of *Macbeth* and *Lear*).

- ❖ *Orlando* by Virginia Woolf (interpreted as a story about Shakespeare's eternal reinvention).

- ❖ *Joy in the Morning* by P. G. Wodehouse (brimful of allusions to *Macbeth*).

- ❖ *The Talented Mr Ripley* by Patricia Highsmith (also influenced by *Macbeth*).

- ❖ *Nothing Like the Sun* by Anthony Burgess (a fictional, bawdy romp through Shakespeare's love life).

- ❖ *The Black Prince* by Iris Murdoch (*Hamlet*).

- ❖ *A Thousand Acres* by Jane Smiley (a direct retelling of *King Lear*).

- ❖ *Lords and Ladies* by Terry Pratchett (based on *A Midsummer Night's Dream*).

- ❖ *Gertrude and Claudius* by John Updike (*Hamlet*).

- ❖ *Lunar Park* by Bret Easton Ellis (a modern-day mash-up of *Hamlet* and *The Tempest*).

Virginia Woolf commented in her 1930 diary: 'I never yet knew how amazing his stretch & speed & word coining power is, until I felt it utterly outpace & outrace my own, seeming to start equal & then I see him draw ahead & do things I could not in my wildest tumult & utmost press of mind imagine... Why then should anyone else attempt to write.'

Charles Dickens is perhaps Shakespeare's natural heir. He was obsessed with Shakespeare, carrying a volume of the plays round with him at all times, and buying a house because of its associations with Falstaff. There are hundreds of echoes of Shakespeare running through his books, including his depiction of family relationships based on Cordelia and Lear, and his deployment of theatrical-style devices borrowed from the plays.

Jane Austen was regularly likened to Shakespeare (by Tennyson, amongst others, who said, 'in the narrow sphere of life which she delineated, she pictured human characters as truthfully as Shakespeare.') Several of Austen's novels show a clear influence, such as *Sense and Sensibility*, which has similarities to *Measure for Measure*, and *Pride and Prejudice*, whose central relationships and key plot points draw on *Much Ado About Nothing*.

## DID YOU KNOW?

Book titles taken from Shakespeare include *Brave New World*, *The Sound and the Fury*, *The Dogs of War*, *Under the Greenwood Tree*, *Infinite Jest*, *The Fault in Our Stars*, *By the Pricking of My Thumbs*, *Remembrance of Things Past*, *Murder Most Foul* and hundreds more.

## Children's Books

Shakespeare himself often appears as a character in books for children, such as in Susan Cooper's *King of Shadows*, and Antonia Forest's *The Player's Boy* and *The Players and the Rebels*. Books that explore Shakespeare's life from different viewpoints include *Will* and *My Father Had a Daughter: Judith Shakespeare's Tale*, both by Grace Tiffany, and *Shakespeare's Mistress* by Karen Harper. Some books explore untold stories in the plays, such as *Ophelia* by Lisa Klein and *Ariel* by Grace Tiffany.

The *Willy Waggledagger* books by Martin Chatterton are a fun way of introducing children to Shakespeare's world, with their sense of humour and punning titles (*Chew Bee or Not Chew Bee*). Shakespeare's most famous quote is the gift that keeps on giving, pun-wise: Pamela Butchart and Thomas Flintham's *To Wee or Not To Wee* introduces young readers to four of the plays in a light style.

## Poetry

One of John Milton's earliest poems (1630) was 'An Epitaph on the Admirable Dramaticke Poet, W. Shakespeare', published as a tribute in the Second Folio: 'Thou in our wonder and astonishment / Has built thyself a live-long monument.' (There's a lot more and it's very gushing.)

Later poets who wrote about or around Shakespeare, or cited him as an influence, include William Wordsworth, Samuel Taylor Coleridge, Lord Byron, Percy Bysshe Shelley, John Keats, Elizabeth Barrett Browning, Alfred Tennyson, Robert Browning, Thomas Hardy, W. B. Yeats, W. H. Auden and Ted Hughes. John Dryden described him as having 'the largest and most comprehensive soul' of all poets.

Poet and essayist Ralph Waldo Emerson put Shakespeare in a super-league of significant humans in his poem 'The Informing Spirit':

*I am the owner of the sphere,*
*Of the seven stars and the solar year,*
*Of Caesar's hand, and Plato's brain,*
*Of Lord Christ's heart, and Shakespeare's strain.*

You don't have to be a good poet to appreciate Shakespeare. The incomparable William McGonagall, generally acknowledged as the worst poet in British history, surpassed himself with his lines: 'Immortal! William Shakespeare, there's none you can excel, / You have drawn out your characters remarkably well.'

## Drama

All post-Shakespeare playwrights owe him a debt, because he was the first to put real human complexity into the characters on the stage. Three modern playwrights who particularly acknowledged Shakespeare's influence were Bertolt Brecht, whose plays borrow plots but give them a satirical twist; Eugène Ionesco, whose *Macbett* reworks *Macbeth*; and Tom Stoppard, whose now-classic play *Rosencrantz and Guildenstern Are Dead* takes two silent characters in *Hamlet* and imagines events from their point of view.

## MUSIC

The drama and emotion of the plays lend themselves well to opera. There are more than 40 operas based on *The Tempest*, including one written as recently as 2004 by British composer Thomas Adès. Mozart was apparently planning to write a *Tempest* opera but died before work could begin. Three of Verdi's most celebrated operas are based on Shakespeare plays: *Macbeth*, *Otello* and *Falstaff*.

Both Tchaikovsky and Prokofiev were inspired by *Romeo and Juliet* to produce some of their finest works. Other classical composers under his influence include Vaughan Williams (*Three Shakespeare Songs*, based on *The Tempest* and *A Midsummer Night's Dream*), Benjamin Britten (an opera based on *A Midsummer Night's Dream*), Sibelius (incidental music for *The Tempest*), Arthur Sullivan (various pieces for stage productions of Shakespeare) and William Walton (film scores for Olivier's *Hamlet*, *Richard III* and *Henry V*). 'The Wedding March', which has accompanied many brides down the aisle, comes from Mendelssohn's suite of music based on *A Midsummer Night's Dream*.

Musicals include Cole Porter's *Kiss Me, Kate* (based on *The Taming of the Shrew*); Leonard Bernstein's *West Side Story* (a *Romeo and Juliet* update), set in 1950s New York, with two rival gangs; plus Elton John and Tim Rice's *The Lion King* (*Hamlet*).

In the world of jazz, Duke Ellington's *Such Sweet Thunder* is an album of tracks based on Shakespeare's work. In pop, Bob Dylan references both Romeo and Ophelia in 'Desolation Row', and the Smiths quote from *Richard III* in 'Cemetery Gates'. The Beatles spliced a radio performance of *King Lear* into 'I Am the Walrus'. Elvis quotes from the 'All the world's a stage' speech from *As You Like It* in 'Are You Lonesome Tonight?'. *Macbeth* has inspired John Cale and Elvis Costello; *Hamlet* and other plays were riffed around by B. A. Robertson in 'To Be or Not To Be'; while *Romeo and Juliet* features in the titles of songs by artists such as Dire Straits and Lou Reed.

Indeed, *Romeo and Juliet* is often used as inspiration, presumably because, like 99.9 per cent of pop songs, it's about young love. The lovers are referenced in 'Fever' (sung best by Peggy Lee), 'Cherish' by Madonna, '(Don't Fear) The Reaper' by Blue Öyster Cult, My Chemical Romance's 'The Sharpest Lives' and the Arctic Monkeys' 'I Bet You Look Good on the Dancefloor', amongst many others.

## FILM

*The Guinness Book of Records* lists Shakespeare as the most-filmed author of all time. It estimates that there have been 79 film versions of *Hamlet* and 52 of *Romeo and Juliet*. The Internet Movie Database (IMDb) gives Shakespeare credits on 1,153 films and TV series, including some which are currently being filmed or in post-production. Not bad going when you died almost 300 years before film came along! If you haven't watched any Shakespeare films, or have been put off by lumbering stagy adaptations, you might like to try some of my favourites:

❖ Kenneth Branagh's charming *Henry V*, with a two-men-and-a-dog cast but a terrifically stirring rendition of the 'St Crispin's Day' battle speech.

❖ Branagh's breezy, funny, visually beautiful *Much Ado About Nothing*. Michael Keaton as Dogberry, pretending to be on a horse, is the weirdest thing ever seen on film, and Keanu Reeves is a woodenly grumpy Don John.

- ❖ Paul Scofield in Peter Brook's *King Lear* (1971), considered one of the best Lears on film.

- ❖ Orson Welles's *Chimes at Midnight* (1965), which is actually scenes and dialogue from several plays about Falstaff, with Welles as the larger-than-life fellow, the role he was born to play. The battle scene, showing Falstaff's ragged army confronting knights on horseback, is terrifying even 50 years on.

- ❖ Mel Gibson's accessible performance in *Hamlet* (1990), directed by Franco Zeffirelli, which comes in at a perfectly reasonable 2 hours and 15 minutes.

- ❖ *10 Things I Hate About You* (1999), based on *The Taming of the Shrew*, which is set in a modern-day high school. It has a witty script, great performances from Heath Ledger and Julia Stiles, and is a total laugh.

- ❖ *Othello* (1995) starring Laurence Fishburne in the title role – unbelievably the first black actor to play Othello in a major film version – and Kenneth Branagh (no getting away from him!) as Iago.

- ❖ Baz Luhrmann's sparkling *William Shakespeare's Romeo + Juliet*, with Claire Danes and Leonardo DiCaprio perfectly cast as the young lovers. It uses the original text in a modern setting with such verve that it totally works. Ah, that swoon-some moment when they see each other at the ball for the first time!

- ❖ Michael Fassbender's *Macbeth* (2016) is gritty and authentic, and suitably bloody.

- ❖ For a film about the man himself it's hard to beat the witty, Oscar-laden *Shakespeare in Love*. Like Shakespeare himself, the film's writers (who included Tom Stoppard) were not sticklers for the facts. But the scenes of London, particularly those on the Thames, bring the era wonderfully to life. Set around the writing of *Romeo and Juliet*, it's good to see a portrayal of Shakespeare with properly inky fingers.

## ACTING

From David Garrick to Laurence Olivier, Shakespeare has always been a way of marking out an actor's career. Starting with Romeo and ending with Lear or Prospero, a talented actor will hope to take in Hamlet, Macbeth, Richard III and Henry V on the way. Olivier, in a classic outburst of luvvie-ness, once said: 'I should be soaring away with my head tilted slightly toward the gods, feeding on the caviar of Shakespeare... An actor must act.'

Women who start out as Juliet tend to progress to Rosalind or Portia, before moving on to Cleopatra, Gertrude or Lady Macbeth. Actress Dame Ellen Terry once exclaimed: 'Have you ever thought how much we all, and women especially, owe to Shakespeare for his vindication of woman in these fearless, high-spirited, resolute and intelligent heroines?' But the peak of Ellen Terry's career was in the late 1800s, and our expectations of parity have moved on since then. None of the female roles comes close to matching the amount of speechifying available to the chaps (Cleopatra and Rosalind are best in terms of sheer volume, but are still more than 150 speeches behind Hamlet). These days, the classic male roles are available to top actresses. Sarah Bernhardt was ahead of her time when she played Hamlet in 1899; more recent actresses such as Frances de la Tour and Maxine Peake have followed, playing Hamlet in 1979 and 2014 respectively. Helen Mirren and Vanessa Redgrave have played Prospero; Harriet Walter has been

Henry IV; and Fiona Shaw and Cate Blanchett have played Richard II.

The part of Hamlet is the Holy Grail for an actor. One reason why it's such a coveted role is that an individual and personalised interpretation is absolutely essential to its success. Oscar Wilde said of Hamlet's incredible malleability: 'there is no such thing as Shakespeare's Hamlet... There are as many Hamlets as there are melancholies.' More recently, theatre critic Michael Billington said much the same thing: 'No actor can ever quite fail as Hamlet... the character is so multi-faceted, it is bound to coincide at some point with an actor's particular gifts.'

---

## DID YOU KNOW?

In 1953 Winston Churchill went to see Richard Burton play Hamlet at the Old Vic. Burton later described how Churchill sat in the front row and said the lines along with him. There was 'this extraordinary rumble,' Burton recalled. 'I could not shake him off. I tried going fast, I tried going slow... During "To be or not to be" he was with me to the death.'

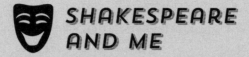

# SHAKESPEARE AND ME

*Nicky Hand is a Digital Media Officer, acting as a guardian of the Shakespeare Birthplace Trust's online presence with her work on their websites, social media and more.*

### What was your switch-on moment?

Studying *The Tempest* for A level. I wasn't sold on it at first but I was lucky enough to have a very passionate teacher. She helped me see beyond the basic storyline and empathise with even the more complex characters. After that I was hooked.

### Which is your favourite of Shakespeare's plays?

It's really hard to pick just one, but probably *The Winter's Tale*. I like a play that evokes your emotions and this one's got the lot! Shakespeare puts you through the wringer with betrayal, tragedy and remorse, then brings you out the other side with some good old-fashioned romance and redemption.

### Tell us about the most memorable performance you've seen.

Trevor Nunn's *King Lear* at the RSC (2007). Ian McKellen was utterly convincing, and I loved the way the set crumbled and deteriorated as

Lear lost his family, his power and his mind. The whole production gave me a new sympathy for the character.

**Which Shakespeare character would you most like to meet?**

Paulina (from *The Winter's Tale*). It's good to see a female character displaying huge strength as well as maternal instinct, and without any lust for power. Paulina stands up to the King at great personal risk because she knows it's the right thing to do. She's the sole voice of reason in a court paralysed by fear and jealous rage, and I'd like to buy that woman a drink.

**How would you persuade somebody to give Shakespeare a chance?**

If you like stories about people, there's something for you to love in Shakespeare. You might need to try more than one play before you find it, but trust me, it'll be there somewhere. It can also help to point out some of the modern adaptations that are based on Shakespeare. If you enjoyed *10 Things I Hate About You*, *House of Cards* or *The Lion King* then you already did give Shakespeare a chance. So what's stopping you seeing some more?

# PART THREE

# SHAKESPEARE, POLITICS AND HUMANITY

## POLITICS

Shakespeare's limitless flexibility and richness mean he has been appropriated by everyone, from Nazis to communists, socialists to Tories, dictators to freedom fighters. Karl Marx quoted from *Timon of Athens* in *Das Kapital*; Hitler referenced 'To be or not to be' in *Mein Kampf*. In the UK in 2003, Nicholas Hytner's *Henry V* at the National took on the troubled feelings around the Iraq war.

As always, much of Shakespeare's eternal appeal is in the infinite variety of interpretations.

That he can be played politically in almost any way has been of great importance in countries where dissent is hard to express. In places such as communist Russia or East Germany, where plays by new writers were often censored, Shakespeare was considered acceptable by the state, allowing him to be widely performed, but it was easy to play his work subversively, sending strong political messages against the regime. In Romania, for instance, under Ceauşescu, Hamlet's Elsinore was portrayed symbolically as a decaying museum.

While some of the plays may have lost their bite for Western audiences, cultures which still practise arranged marriage or prohibit the mingling of races and religions will find urgent relevance in *Romeo and Juliet*. Journalist Yasmin Alibhai-Brown, a Muslim, has spoken movingly of how playing Juliet in a mixed-race version of *Romeo and Juliet* at her school in

Uganda, opposite a black Romeo, resulted in her father never speaking to her again.

Many great statesmen have loved Shakespeare. Abraham Lincoln read his works aloud many evenings to his aides (one can only hope the aides were equally keen). Churchill, when he wasn't reciting *Hamlet* along with Richard Burton, liked to weave Shakespeare quotations into his speeches and other communications. In his famous 'Their Finest Hour' speech in 1940, for example, there were conscious echoes of *Henry V*. After hearing Olivier's morale-boosting 'St Crispin's Day' speech on the radio near the start of World War Two, Churchill asked Olivier to produce a film version, which he duly did. And in a memo to his staff in 1943, Churchill concluded with a rousing quote from *Julius Caesar*, the one which begins, 'There is a tide in the affairs of men...'

## PRISONERS

Many prisoners report that Shakespeare helped them through their ordeal. One such was the French soldier Alfred Dreyfus, accused of treason in the late nineteenth century (the notorious 'Dreyfus affair'). During his time in prison on Devil's Island, Dreyfus taught himself to read Shakespeare in the original English, finding parallels to his own situation within the plays. P. G. Wodehouse was a prisoner in World War Two, arrested by the Gestapo at his French home in 1940 and held captive for almost a year. Given very little time to get some things together, he chose – in addition to underwear, tobacco and tea – his copy of Shakespeare.

Most famously, the South African political prisoners on Robben Island talked after their release about how a smuggled copy of the *Complete Works*, disguised as a Hindu Bible, was passed round. Each of them signed their names by their favourite passages. Walter Sisulu chose a speech of Shylock's: 'Still have I borne it with a patient shrug, / For suff'rance is the badge of all our tribe.' Nelson Mandela chose the passage from *Julius Caesar* which begins, 'Cowards die many times before their deaths; / The valiant never taste of death but once.' Mandela said years later, 'Shakespeare always seems to have something to say to us.'

## THE INVENTION OF THE HUMAN

Taking his archetypal, living, breathing characters as a starting point – Hamlet, Richard III, Romeo, Lady Macbeth – philosophers and thinkers have explored what Shakespeare teaches us about our own humanity, from Nietzsche ('Shakespeare reflected a great deal on the passions and from his temperament probably had very intimate access to many of them (dramatists are in general somewhat wicked men)') to Goethe (on having seen one of the plays, he said he felt 'like a blind man given the gift of sight').

Dr Samuel Johnson, who compiled an eighteenth-century edition of the plays, spoke rather disapprovingly of some facets of Shakespeare. Yet the modern reader might think the criticisms read rather more like praise: 'He... is so much more careful to please than to instruct, that he seems to write without any moral purpose... he makes no just distribution of good or evil, nor is always careful to shew in the virtuous a disapprobation of the wicked; he carries his persons indifferently through right and wrong...' As a writer, I wouldn't mind someone saying that about me.

Sigmund Freud regarded Hamlet as a perfect case study to explore the concept of the unconscious, being one of the first characters in literature to be a fully realised human wracked with doubt, inner conflicts and suicidal thoughts. Freud also used him to illustrate the Oedipus complex, theorising that Hamlet is tormented by guilt and indecision when contemplating killing Claudius because Claudius has only gone and done what he, Hamlet, subconsciously wished to do, namely kill his father and sleep with his mother. Many theatrical interpretations of *Hamlet* since Freud's day have seized upon this intriguing angle as a way of casting a young attractive woman to play Hamlet's mother Gertrude.

Ludwig Wittgenstein was less impressed by Shakespeare, finding some of the work hard to understand. And he was definitely not a fan of the fans, saying, 'I am *deeply* suspicious of most of Shakespeare's admirers.' It's likely then, had he gained access to a time machine, Wittgenstein would have been very deeply suspicious of Harold Bloom.

Bloom, an American literary critic, is happy to admit to being a Shakespeare obsessive: 'I preach Bardolatry as the most benign of all religions' and, more baldly, making David Garrick appear lukewarm, 'Shakespeare is God'. Bloom argues in *Shakespeare: The Invention of the Human* that Shakespeare created something that hadn't existed before: personality, or what it means to be human. In particular, he notes how Shakespeare shows characters reflecting on their actions, 'overhearing' themselves in the soliloquies and determining to change. By these means, Bloom claims that Shakespeare not only showed us new ways to understand ourselves, but also new ways to be.

---

## DID YOU KNOW?

Almost all the moons of Uranus are named after characters from Shakespeare, including Titania, Oberon, Puck, Prospero, Caliban and Rosalind.

# PART FOUR
# SHAKESPEARE
# AND LANGUAGE

There are two key reasons why Shakespeare has such staying power. One is his sublime and complex characters; the other is the way he put words together. Few writers have wielded their pen – or quill – with such power and originality, and his mastery of the language still inspires awe in us today.

## WORDSMITHERY

It's often said that Shakespeare coined many new words. It's not quite clear, though, how many were his creations, and how many were already in use but had not yet been written down. The contemporary critic Francis Meres commented in 1598 on how various poets and writers, including Shakespeare, Marlowe and six others, had enriched English with 'rare ornaments'. This does suggest that these chaps were responsible for some of the word-coining and phrase-making. Of course, they were writing in the early days of print and were filling shelves that were fairly bare. Certainly, in the 150 years between 1500 and 1650, something in the order of 12,000 new words entered the English language.

Shakespeare's plays contain the first known examples of a great many words – it used to be thought around 1,700 or so – but recent technological advances in digitising old texts have revealed that some words the *Oxford English Dictionary* cites as being of Shakespearean origin actually appeared earlier.

Though plenty of the words he first used were never heard again ('congreet' or 'rigol', anyone?), several hundred, perhaps as many as 800, are still used today. 'Useful', 'excitement', 'fashionable' and 'hurry' are amongst the countless new words he introduced. (Actually, 'countless' is one of his too.) As are 'bloodstained', 'eyeball', 'addiction', 'critic', 'mountaineer' and 'gossip'.

Shakespeare also did a lot of attaching *un-* to words that hadn't previously been used in that way, such as 'uncomfortable', 'unchanging', 'undress', 'uneducated' and 'unreal' (the *Oxford English Dictionary* lists 38 of them).

Some people are put off Shakespeare by what they see as the insurmountably difficult obstacle of the language. Yet about 95 per cent of his words are still in use today. Admittedly, he was fond of 'thou' instead of 'you', though it was already a bit out of date. And sometimes a word we know had a different meaning back then. For instance, 'doubt' meant 'fear', 'table' meant 'notebook', and 'lover' sometimes meant 'dear friend'. And because pronunciation has changed over the centuries, some of the rhymes don't work any more. For example, 'bone' and 'gone', 'swears' and 'tears', 'remove' and 'love' would have rhymed with each other. These rhymes are restored by theatre companies that perform the plays in 'original pronunciation', such as Ben Crystal's troupe Passion in Practice. This allows the words to be heard as they would have been in Shakespeare's day.

Some of the speeches can be a bit flowery, because with limited or non-existent stage sets, audiences would have relied on actors' words to tell them what to see and imagine. (That's why the language can sometimes seem over the top in a film that pulls out all the scenery stops.) But Shakespeare often uses very simple language when the chips are down. For instance, in *Macbeth*, when Macduff learns that his wife and children have been slaughtered, he cannot take it in, and keeps asking, 'All my pretty ones? / Did you say all?', and a moment later, 'What, all my pretty chickens?' And it doesn't get much simpler or more heartfelt than Henry V wooing Katherine: 'I know no ways to mince it in love, but directly to say, "I love you".'

Despite – but also because of – the language, the emotion travels down the wires from four-hundred-and-something years ago, and hits us right between the eyes.

---

## DID YOU KNOW?

Shakespeare invented the knock-knock joke:
'Knock, knock, knock. Who's there?'
(*Macbeth*)

---

## PHRASE-MAKING

Shakespeare was a terrific phrase-maker – probably the greatest there has ever been. It's because of him that we say 'catch a cold', 'naked truth' and 'green-eyed monster'. Just a few of the hundreds of his phrases that we still use today are in the table below.

He was an absolute master of insults as well: 'You scullion, you rampallian, you fustilarian! I'll tickle your catastrophe!' Or the unbeatable 'There's no more faith in thee than in a stewed prune' (Falstaff).

## DID YOU KNOW?

'What the dickens' has nothing to do with Charles Dickens. It's one of Shakespeare's, from *The Merry Wives of Windsor*. Dickens is a euphemism for 'devil'.

| PHRASE-MAKER | |
|---|---|
| Shakespeare's ability to whip up a memorable phrase was second to none. 'Second to none' is one of his, funnily enough, as are: | |
| All Greek to me | As merry as the day is long |
| Bated breath | Be cruel to be kind |
| Breathing one's last | Budge an inch |
| Cold comfort | Dead as a doornail |
| Eaten out of house and home | Faint-hearted |
| Fair play | Fast and loose |
| Foregone conclusion | Foul play |

| | |
|---|---|
| Full circle | Heart of gold |
| High time | In a pickle |
| In my mind's eye | It's all one to me |
| Lie low | Milk of human kindness |
| More in sorrow than in anger | Short shrift |
| Spotless reputation | Tongue-tied |
| Too much of a good thing | Tower of strength |
| Truth will out | Vanish into thin air |

# 'GIVE ME NOW LEAVE TO LEAVE THEE'

And so 'Our revels now are ended', as Prospero says. Often it seems as if Shakespeare is everywhere: from the books we read, to the words we use, rippling through our films and politics, and even the way we think about ourselves. I hope this book was as you like it, and that it has perhaps inspired you to see a play or read a poem – again or for the first time. And if not, well, there's no more faith in thee than in a stewed prune. Ha! I *knew* I'd be using that soon.

# RESOURCES

## BOOKS

Although there are uncountable numbers of books on Shakespeare, I found these ones particularly invaluable:

❖ Bate, Jonathan *The Genius of Shakespeare* (2016, Picador). Fascinating, erudite and eye-opening account of how Shakespeare came to be regarded as the greatest ever writer.

❖ Bryson, Bill *Shakespeare: The World as Stage* (2008, HarperCollins). Written with Bryson's trademark lightness of touch, this is a great intro to Shakespeare's life and times. There are newer (and illustrated) editions too.

❖ Crystal, Ben *Shakespeare on Toast: Getting a Taste for the Bard* (2009, Icon Books). Utterly accessible and fun guide to Shakespeare's language and how to get more out of watching the plays.

❖ Dickson, Andrew *The Rough Guide to Shakespeare* (2009, Rough Guides). Invaluable, thorough, intelligent guide to the plays (and more). Now in a new form, *The Globe Guide to Shakespeare*.

❖ Gross, John (editor) *After Shakespeare: Writing Inspired by the World's Greatest Author* (2002, Oxford University Press). Contains what just about every well-known person has ever said about Shakespeare, and includes writings inspired by his work.

❖ Shapiro, James *Contested Will: Who Wrote Shakespeare?* (2010, Faber & Faber). Thoughtful and thorough analysis of the authorship controversy, which ends up revealing an awful lot about human nature along the way.

❖ Wells, Stanley *William Shakespeare: A Very Short Introduction* (2015, Oxford University Press). An astonishing amount of useful information from one of the top Shakespeare experts, packed into a handy pocket-sized book. Highly readable.

The following will provide background colour:

❖ Nicholl, Charles *The Lodger: Shakespeare on Silver Street* (2008, Penguin).

❖ O'Reilly, Sally *Dark Aemilia: A Novel of Shakespeare's Dark Lady* (2014, Myriad Editions).

❖ Paterson, Don (editor) *101 Sonnets* (2002, Faber & Faber).

❖ Sher, Antony *Year of the King* (2004, Nick Hern Books).

'There are hundreds more fine books on Shakespeare,' says the Modern Library website, who give their own list at **modernlibrary.com/2010/09/14/100-of-the-best-books-on-shakespeare**.

## WEBSITES

Google Shakespeare's name and you get 131,000,000 hits. Sometimes it felt like I'd looked at all of them. Here are the websites I bookmarked:

❖ SparkNotes is solidly reliable for plot summaries of plays and character information: **sparknotes.com**.

❖ The full texts of the plays are available on MIT's site, **shakespeare.mit.edu**. They also have a related site, **globalshakespeares.mit.edu**, which has an archive of video clips of Shakespeare plays, films and TV programmes, some of which are mentioned in this book.

❖ I really enjoyed flicking through the Bodleian Library's virtual facsimile of the First Folio: **firstfolio.bodleian.ox. ac.uk**.

❖ For tweet-sized summaries of the plays, the Reduced Shakespeare Company have archived theirs here: **reducedshakespeare.com/2009/11/tweeting-shakespeare**. Sample tweet, for *King Lear*: 'It's hell getting old.'

❖ The terrific **shakespeareswords.com** is a web-based edition of the book of the same name by David and Ben Crystal. Searching for just about anything is really easy.

❖ I made great use of **opensourceshakespeare.org**, which has separate sections for characters, plays and poems. It also has a concordance, where you can search for any word that Shakespeare used and it will tell you how many times he used it and where. It makes you feel sorry for pre-internet Shakespeare scholars, to be honest.

❖ The Folger Shakespeare Library website is a great archive of facts and figures, but also has links to some interesting podcasts about Shakespeare: **folger.edu/shakespeare**.

## APPS

The Shakespeare Pro® app contains the *Complete Works*, plus play summaries, glossaries and loads more. All right there on your phone, so you can look stuff up wherever you are. Genuinely useful.

## PLACES TO VISIT

The mother ship for the eager Shakespeare fan is of course Stratford-upon-Avon (make sure not to confuse it with Stratford in East London). You can visit Shakespeare's birthplace, Anne Hathaway's Cottage, Mary Arden's Farm and Hall's Croft, where his daughter Susanna lived. New Place, the house Shakespeare bought when he'd made a few bob, was torn down in the eighteenth century, but the Shakespeare Birthplace Trust are involved (at the time of writing) in a project to reimagine how it and the garden would have looked. You can also visit Shakespeare's grave in Holy Trinity Church, just a short walk from the Royal Shakespeare Company Theatre, where you can, of course, take in a play or two.

In London, the Globe Theatre exhibition and tour is well worth a visit. You get to go inside the theatre itself and see what an extraordinary achievement its reconstruction was. While you're there, you might be able to watch a play later that day. At £5 for a standing ticket, watching a play at the Globe is something that's available to everyone.

# ACKNOWLEDGEMENTS

I'd first like to thank the people whose interviews you can read in this book, who were all very generous with their time. In particular, Ben Crystal, Charles Nicholl, Jo Shapcott and Andrew Wincott good-naturedly answered my many additional questions about Shakespeare – I decided I might as well capitalise on their expertise while I'd got their attention. They were not only helpful and enlightening in their answers, but contagious in their enthusiasm. Professor Michael Dobson, another interviewee, wrote the wonderful foreword which graces the start of this book. David Bellwood from the Globe, also an interviewee, arranged for me to have a tour there, which was wonderful. Caroline Durbin at the Shakespeare Birthplace Trust was incredibly kind and helpful at arranging interviews with Trust people, and I am extremely grateful to Sir Stanley Wells of the Trust, for reading the book and providing us with a lovely quote for the cover. Sue Powell, Sir Antony Sher's assistant, was also really kind and responsive.

It was, once again, a great pleasure working with the lovely people of Summersdale, especially the onlie begetter Abbie Headon, and Robert Drew, who are both funny, smart and super-efficient.

I benefitted hugely from the advice, wisdom and expertise of my friends: in particular, Chris Winterflood, the poet, who lives a stone's throw from the Globe; storyteller Sam Knowles; and Trish Joscelyne, an expert on children's literature. Talking of children, mine were very enthusiastic about the book. Twelve-year-old Mol, who has been in *A Midsummer Night's Dream*, remembered all the mechanicals' names, and ten-year-old Saul sat through the film of *Much Ado About Nothing* and hardly complained. I would especially like to thank John, my husband, whose support, immense knowledge of history and literature, and boundless reserves of good humour made this a thoroughly enjoyable book to work on.

A CELEBRATION OF THE
WORLD'S FINEST MUSIC

FOR THE LOVE OF
CLASSICAL
MUSIC

A COMPANION

CAROLINE HIGH

FOR THE LOVE OF CLASSICAL MUSIC

Caroline High

ISBN: 978-1-84953-732-2

Hardback

£9.99

From Bach to Beethoven, Vivaldi to Vaughan Williams, the world of classical music has something to enchant every listener. Whether you're an armchair connoisseur, a regular concert-goer or an ardent musician, *For the Love of Classical Music* will take you on a tour encompassing landmark pieces and performances, key artists and composers, and surprising facts about the world's most beautiful music.

FOR THE LOVE OF
RADIO 4

AN UNOFFICIAL
COMPANION

CAROLINE HODGSON

FOR THE LOVE OF RADIO 4

Caroline Hodgson

ISBN: 978-1-84953-642-4

Hardback

£9.99

From *Farming Today* at sunrise to the gentle strains of 'Sailing By' and the Shipping Forecast long after midnight, Radio 4 provides the soundtrack to life for millions of Britons. In *For the Love of Radio 4*, Caroline Hodgson celebrates all that's best about the nation's favourite spoken-word station, taking us on a tour through its history, its key personalities and programmes, and countless memorable moments from the archives.

*'I found the book to be full of fascinating detail. It is clearly a labour of love, perfectly designed for Radio 4 lovers.'*

Simon Brett

*'If you love Radio 4 it's impossible to turn it off. If you read this book it's impossible to put down.'*

Charles Collingwood

If you're interested in finding out more about our books,
find us on Facebook at **Summersdale Publishers** and
follow us on Twitter at **@Summersdale**.

# www.summersdale.com